MISSIONARY WARRIOR

MISSIONARY WARRIOR

NEWLY REVISED EDITION

LETTIE B. COWMAN

OMS · ONE MISSION SOCIETY

By God's grace, One Mission Society unites, inspires, and equips Christians to make disciples of Jesus Christ, multiplying dynamic communities of believers around the world.

One Mission Society is an evangelical, interdenominational faith mission that multiplies disciples, churches, missionary movements, and leaders around the world.

One Mission Society
PO Box A
Greenwood, IN 46142
317.888.3333
www.onemissionsociety.org
http://oms.media
Missionary Warrior – Lettie B. Cowman
Copyright © 2019 by One Mission Society
Paperback ISBN: 978-1-62245-629-1
eBook ISBN: 978-1-62245-630-7
Cover design by Jonathan Lewis

Scripture quotations are taken from the Holy Bible, King James Version, Cambridge, 1769.

All rights reserved. No part of this book may be reproduced in any form without permission in writing from the publisher, except in the case of brief quotations in critical articles or reviews.

BIOGRAPHY & AUTOBIOGRAPHY / Religious

Printed in the United States of America

10 9 8 7 6 5 4 3 2 1

Contents

Foreword ix
Ch. 1: In the Beginning 1
Ch. 2: A New Affection 15
Ch. 3: Another Life Crisis 27
Ch. 4: The Volunteer 31
Ch. 5: The Call 37
Ch. 6: Launching Forth 47
Ch. 7: Evangelistic Tours 71
Ch. 8: Enlarged Borders 83
Ch. 9: The Promotion of Scriptural Holiness 91
Ch. 10: The Advance Into Korea 97
Ch. 11: Deputation Tours 103
Ch. 12: The Call to China 117
Ch. 13: The Great Village Campaign 121
Ch. 14: Music in the Solitudes 139
Ch. 15: In the Thickening Shadows 151
Ch. 16: The Afterglow of a Sunlit Life 161
Epilogue 169
Photos 171
Other Similar Titles 179

Foreword

"True biography," someone said, "was never nor can ever be written. Fragrance cannot be put into picture or poem. There is a subtle, evasive savor and flavor about character, which escapes both tongue and pen. And, more than this, the very best things about such characters and careers are unknown, except to God, and these cannot be revealed because they are among his secret things. Like Elijah, the best men hide themselves with God before they show themselves to men."[1]

What pen can fully compass or adequately portray the story of simple faith and mighty achievement, of faithful and heroic service of the subject of this memoir, Charles Cowman, the missionary whose life literally burned out, the man whose master passion was missions? Such a life has a message for our day.

As he served Christ, so also ought we to serve him, and surely, we will serve him better as we see what a noble service was rendered by this missionary. To young people his message was always, "Find God's plan for your generation and get in line with it."

This volume has, like the life it sketches, just one purpose. It is simply and solely meant not to exalt a personality but to

---

[1] Rev. Arthur T. Pierson, D.D., ed., Missionary Review of the World, 1906.

show the reader what God can do with a humble instrument when fully and completely yielded to him. He needs no praise for his work, but we need the motivation that his consecrated example gave to the world. Neither life nor labor has been in vain. What marvels may be wrought by the inspiration of a single life!

In this work, I would beg indulgence for many shortcomings of which I am painfully conscious. I have tried to paint impartially the portrait of my beloved husband as he lived, and if in any measure I have conveyed the lesson that a life wholly surrendered to God is the life that wins, I have not wholly failed in my task.

Lettie B. Cowman
Los Angeles, California
September 25, 1928

Chapter 1

In the Beginning

In faded writing in the Cowman family Bible are the names of George W. Cowman, born October 16, 1810, and Elizabeth, his wife, born July 27, 1820.

George's parents, a mixture of English and Scottish, came from Great Britain in the late 18th century and settled in the South. The few preserved records give glimpses of life on an old southern plantation.

George was the eldest of a large family. He migrated northward to seek his fortune in a newer and thriftier country. Years later, he would take his children on his knee and relate to them stories of his boyhood days, of the tearful parting from his parents and sisters, the long wagon journey over rough roads and through swollen streams, and the warm hospitality of the northerners.

North and South joined hands when he met Elizabeth. Their honeymoon was spent on a long pioneer journey to Illinois, where they prayed for their new home, "May it be to us as the house of God and the gate of heaven."

Their neighbors were kindhearted, fairly well-educated men and women with ideals of righteousness and truth; the pioneer community might have been termed *Christian*. Their surroundings at all times challenged the courage of the bravest, but all was not dreariness. By the evening light of the fire they read Dickens, Whittier, and Shakespeare.

Every year, new settlers came; all were heartily welcomed. There were many housewarmings and husking bees as well as a rare type of hospitality, as the neighbors were acquainted with each other from Hickory Hill to Four Mile Creek.

God gave George and Elizabeth nine children. David Franklin was the second child and greatly loved by his mother. He was fond of books and possessed a gift for teaching, so his parents did their utmost to give him a good education. From his earliest youth, he was a leader among the young people. When George died and left Elizabeth with the family to raise, she looked to David for counsel.

What a mother Elizabeth was! Every bit of cooking and baking had to be done by her own hands. She had to weave cloth on a hand loom and make clothing without a sewing machine. However, every Sunday morning she was present at church with all her family neatly clad in their homespun. Her children said of her, "We never saw our mother lose her temper or heard her speak a harsh word." What was the secret? Her faith was in God, and she leaned upon his strong arm.

The nearest neighbors were the congenial, hospitable John Keyes family, staunch Presbyterians. John and Sarah Keyes had three sons and one daughter, Mary. When Mary was only 13, her mother died. From then on, much of the care of the home rested upon her.

The neighbors considered her an unusual character; they loved her and called her "our Mary." She was always spotlessly clean with her jet-black hair neatly braided. She attended school during autumn and winter months, and by age 17, she possessed a thorough education for her day. Along with her studies, she learned the art of homemaking and became an ideal housekeeper.

The Cowman and Keyes families practically grew up together. They attended the same school and church, and David was often at the Keyes' home where there were boys his own age; however, there was another magnet drawing him there.

When their teen years ended, David and Mary dreamed of a home of their own, but their dreams were cut short by the Civil War. Thousands enlisted, including David, who volunteered for service under Company G, 83rd Illinois Infantry, in August 1861.

From 1861 to 1864, the nation became weary and heartsick of the long, drawn-out struggle. David and Mary exchanged letters, and she often read and reread them, then tied them with a bit of ribbon and placed them carefully away. On Sundays, at the little log church, they offered prayer for the safety of the loved ones on the front line.

One sweltering August day, Company G was ordered out on a long march through mountainous terrain. The air was stifling. David fell by the wayside, quite overcome. The enemy was in hot pursuit, and no one had time to pick him up. But one kindhearted soldier lifted him up, laid him under a tree, and marched on.

A few hours later, another company came along the same route. In this company was Henry Cowman, David's brother. He noticed a soldier lying under a tree and felt irresistibly drawn to step aside to see who it was. There, he recognized his own brother. He pressed his canteen to David's lips, and soon he revived and was able to return to his own camp. Thus, the life of David Cowman was spared.

As the fourth year of the war ended, news that thrilled the hearts of all flashed over the wires: Peace had been declared. Company G received orders to return home.

Five months later, on September 21, 1865, David led Mary to the marriage altar. It was a glorious autumn day with a touch of Indian summer in the air. The bride was lovely in her dress of soft gray with its trim-fitting bodice and sleeves of lace. Her skirt measured six full yards around the bottom with an added fluting and shirring, every stitch made by the bride herself. How often over the years did Mother Cowman sit by the firelight and describe that wonderful wedding day; she would name the friends who were present, dwelling on the beautiful traits of her young husband and recalling the new home where they began life together.

Their first home near Toulon, Illinois, stood on a picturesque knoll overlooking woodland and meadows. During the winter, David taught school, and in the summer, he took care of the farm. On August 1, 1866, Cora Esther was born, and on March 13, 1868, their joy was complete when their little black-eyed son, Charles Elmer, was born.

For a while, the day of his birth seemed likely to prove the day of his death. Evidence of life was so slight that, at first, he was laid aside as dead. But soon, one of the attendants noticed a slight heaving of the chest. Baby Charles emitted a low cry, and thus a life was saved that proved to be of incalculable value to the world.

When he was only two weeks old, his parents dedicated him to God's service, claimed promises, and wrote his name across the best of them, though not knowing what the future held for him. How often, in the twilight hours when all alone, Mary prayed, "Oh, God, help my boy to grow up to be a good and useful man!"

Charles' lullabies were old-fashioned hymns. As far back as they could trace, on both sides of his ancestry, lay generations of clean and virtuous Christians whose beliefs were tangible possessions to them. They gave him a sound body, a dauntless spirit, a venturesome mind, and resourceful courage.

David and Mary Cowman expected to make the training of their children the supreme business of their lives, and they prayed for divine guidance as they began to plan. Should they move to the city for more educational advantages? Might the allurements there be more than they could resist? When the way seemed clear, they moved to a place that afforded better advantages but still kept them in the great open country. In later years, they would truly testify that the hand of God was upon them and led them in the right way. Mary often said, "It was the best of moves. We brought our children up by themselves and with us, as we never could have done in the city, so they were saved the dangers and difficulties that they might not have been strong enough to meet."

A strange incident occurred during their move from Illinois to Iowa in the springtime of 1870. They arrived one evening at a place near Thayer, Iowa, known as the Burd Estate. The large house was a landmark for travelers. Isaac and Margaret Burd, Philadelphians, were among the early settlers in that region. They often entertained strangers, and the Cowman family spent the night under their hospitable roof.

As it happened, the Burd Estate was my home, and I was there that night – just a three-month-old baby girl named Lettie. Little Charles Cowman was only two years old. Did God whisper to the mothers that night that these two children were destined for each other, or did he keep it a secret until later?

In May the whole countryside was unspeakably beautiful – the fields, the hedgerows, the farms, and the cherry trees were in full bloom. Wild flowers draped every knoll with beauty. In a picturesque region 20 miles from the Burd Estate, the Cowmans purchased their farm and established their new home by a river close to a forest. The place was known as The Cedars because of the stately trees that bordered the walk. Flowers grew in neatly kept beds; behind the garden was an orchard with fields of corn, wheat, and meadowland surrounding it. The woods rang with birdsong.

Charles spent his boyhood days in this rural magnificence. His mother made a homey atmosphere about her, and the parents were like two youthful companions to their children. Together, they played, told stories, and walked through the meadows. Charles' great love for God's creation was doubtless implanted in his heart in these early years.

The Cowman family was an integral part of their community, and their hospitable home graciously welcomed friends and strangers alike, having a far-reaching influence. The children were fortunate indeed to be born into a family with neither poverty nor riches, so that they did not experience the temptations of either.

Each day, Cora and Charles trudged along to school more than a mile away. Every night, their father examined them in their studies and watched their progress with vigilance.

In the home, the parents gave religious training first place and did not permit anything to interfere. On Sundays, everyone went to church, and it was never a debatable question whether Charles would go or remain at home. They attended Centenary Methodist Church, a white frame building with a belfry. Every two weeks, a preacher came to hold services. He was filled with the Holy Spirit, and tears ran down his cheeks while he preached. A holy anointing inspired his very tones, which made a lasting impression on the children.

The preacher usually accompanied the Cowmans home for dinner, and then in the evening, all would walk back to church. The Cowman home was known throughout the country as a haven for the early circuit riders. These circuit riders had unique personalities that commanded reverence and appreciation, and those who were permitted to entertain such men of God felt honored.

David Cowman was a Methodist class leader. During the week, as the neighbors gathered in different homes for prayer, testimony, and Scripture reading, God met them in a gracious manner. The Cowmans read the large family Bible daily. Because it held something of reverence and awe, when it was taken down to be read, the children sat listening quietly. This early reading took Charles back and forth through the Scriptures several times. Before he was able to pronounce the long names, he had read the Gospels through and had memorized many portions. These early impressions and influences never left his mind.

When Charles was about 10, a farmer living 20 miles away went to the city, brought home a keg of liquor, and became intoxicated. What consternation this caused! It was talked about in every home. The children were excited as they listened to the comments of their elders who warned them against the deadly drink. Parents prayed around family altars that their children might never taste the poison. Temperance was a strong principle with them.

"Never go into debt" was an adage of the Cowman household. They dreaded debt as much as a contagious disease. This deeply held rule of life made Charles' adult life remarkable.

David Cowman was a man of few words. One of the things his son never could forget was the father's utter sincerity and hatred of everything mean and underhanded. He was the very soul of honor and expected as much from everybody else.

Mary Cowman was the mainspring of Charles' life. They were great companions, and the heart-to-heart talks between the young mother and son laid the foundation of his character. She seemed to draw out all that was chivalrous and manly in a boy's nature. Faithfulness, courtesy, and friendliness developed in her son.

The family spent eight happy years in this home. They passed victoriously through hardships, and life bloomed fair with cherished hopes. Another child, Lillian, had been born. Charles was exceedingly fond of her and loved to carry her about or sit by her cradle and rock her to sleep.

But Lillian suddenly became ill when she was about a year old. After a few days of anxious waiting and helpless watching, she died. When they carried her body away to the cemetery, Charles' heart broke, and he wept uncontrollably beside her grave. *Why* had the God of love taken from them the one whom they loved so tenderly? Was he good to have done such a thing? How God can hurt when he loves was a puzzle to Charles. Rebellion rose in his young heart, but he kept it hidden, not daring to tell his dear mother.

One Sunday morning, the Methodist preacher announced a revival meeting. He asked that all the families pray especially for their children, so that every one of them might be brought into the fold. He said, "We need an awakening."

One night, at the conclusion of the sermon, while the congregation sang, "Come ye sinners, poor and needy, weak and wounded, sick and sore,"[2] Charles, without enticement, left his seat, walked down to the mourners' bench, and wept out his sorrow. The impression of that experience remained with him to the day of his death. A ray of light stole into his young heart, and he seemed to see the Good Shepherd walking through green pastures with a little lamb upon his arm. His kind words quieted all fears as he said, "It is well with your sister, and some day you will meet her again."

Into his heart came a strange peace, a sunburst of revelation. Charles learned that not in cruelty, not in wrath, but in love God had transplanted their loved one to a sunnier place. From that moment, he pictured baby Lillian in the King's palace

---

[2] Joseph Hart, "Come Ye Sinners, Poor and Needy," 1759.

garden. On the way home that winter night, he sang for joy. The terrible tempest that had raged in his young heart was stilled.

The revival was thought by many to have been a failure, as only one boy had been converted. But how little they realized what that conversion would mean to thousands of lost souls. How little did anyone of that community dream that he would someday become a missionary and the founder of one of the great evangelizing forces on earth.

The years of Charles' childhood passed. David and Mary realized that change was inevitable. He had passed his 15th birthday and needed advanced schooling. An unseen hand was leading him forward.

The family moved again. In their new home, a warm friendship sprang up between a young telegraph operator and Charles. He spent many hours in the telegraph office, fascinated by the click of the instruments. During vacation, he studied telegraphy as a pastime. He never meant to make it his profession. But in several months, when he was able to send and receive messages and dispatch trains, a position was offered to him at a railway station some miles from home. He begged his parents to permit him to accept it until the opening of the autumn term of school. Reluctantly they consented, and the boy of 15 cut loose from his moorings and started out upon an unknown sea, which was a marked turning point in his life.

It was the first time he had ever been away from home for a night, and his parents were anxious; they feared he would fall asleep on duty and allow the trains to pass by. But he never slept at his post. He quickly became known from one end of the line to the other as the "boy operator." The trainmen loved him, and the conductors said they had never met a more promising lad.

In this new world, Charles' boyhood days seemed to end, and before him was the hard, serious business of life – the training school for the still greater days ahead. When autumn came, he had no desire to return to school.

My childhood home was a short distance from the village where Charles was the night operator for the railway station. One day, my mother went to the village and on her return home said, "I met a dear lad today. He had such a frank, open countenance, but there is an air of loneliness about him, and I thought he must be away from his home and parents for the first time. When I spoke to him, I found that he was. His name is Charles Cowman. I invited him to the house as I feel he needs a little bit of mothering."

I was a mere school girl, just past my 13th birthday. A small lake and a deep, rolling meadow separated my home from the village school. Morning and evening, I had to cross the steps of the railway station to reach our roadway. From that point on, Charles would often accompany me home, open the heavy meadow gates, and upon Mother's invitation, remain for evening tea. We learned much about his boyhood, and Mother was delighted to know that he was the boy who had spent the night with his family in our home about 13 years before. A lifelong friendship sprang up between our families.

The pupils of Mrs. Barnhart were planning an evening of musical entertainment at the Methodist church in our village. I was one of her pupils and had a part in the program. Nearly every girl on the program had a brother about her own age, but mine were all grown up. The brothers were to march down the aisle with their sisters to the platform. Several days before the entertainment, I received a brief note:

Miss Lettie Burd,

May I have the privilege of accompanying you to the concert on Friday evening?

> Yours sincerely,
> Charles Cowman

Mother consented. That evening, the church was filled, and down the aisle marched the pupils, led by Mrs. Barnhart. Charles and I followed immediately behind her. My dress was snowy white, and I carried an armful of roses. Something whispered to my mother at that moment, "Somewhere through the coming years, your little girl will walk down the aisle with that boy to the marriage altar."

Some weeks later, Charles received a promotion, and he transferred to a division center many miles away. He came at once to tell my mother, but he told me something else. Our parents smiled at our childhood romance and made no objection. From the first time we met, we were sweethearts, and to the last breath he drew, we were sweethearts still.

A year later, another promotion was offered. At 17, he became train dispatcher at one of the largest division centers of the Burlington Railway. At 18, he transferred to Chicago to a still more important position in the railroad office of the same company. Other promotions followed in rapid succession, and he climbed the ladder of success. At age 19, he earned the same salary as employees of many years' standing.

On Sundays, Charles went to church as he had been taught. But the great city congregation seemed entirely different from the humble village meetinghouse. He missed the familiar faces and the cordial manner of his former church friends. He listened to the same sweet hymns and the same Gospel story, but not finding the interest his young heart craved, he returned to his lodging with a touch of genuine homesickness. After a time, his work kept him at his desk on Sundays, and little by little, he neglected church attendance. This soon drifted into indifference, and the voice of God died out in his soul.

Temptations were present, and the city streets were full of allurements. Charles saw many of his young fellow workers wreck their lives through debauchery and drink. However, his early training, the example and prayers of his father and mother, and the overshadowing mercy of God preserved him from the sins of youth. Nevertheless, his parents suffered much anxiety. When an opportunity came for him to become manager of the Western Union Telegraph office at Glenwood Springs, Colorado, they strongly advised the change. He accepted the position.

But even there, he found himself in a strange environment that would have tested and tried many an older person. His dealings were mainly with mining officials who gambled with the mining stock, losing and gaining fortunes overnight. Often, men would slip a bill into his hand, wishing to see some private telegrams that would have let them in on the secret of the daily market. But this honest young man always quietly refused. He had no love of money. He lived in modest lodgings and laid aside enough funds every month with which to purchase a home.

Charles remained in this position until his 21st birthday. Then, on June 8, 1889, our childhood dream was realized; a honeymoon began that increased in joy and love and lasted for 36 years.

We lived in our first home in the heart of the Rockies for several years. It seemed that heaven had begun. We were ideally happy together. But God, whose ways are higher than ours, had to stir up that cozy nest so that his purpose for the future might be carried out. The altitude proved too high for me, and several times it looked as if life itself would flicker out. Once, as the doctor tried to find my feeble pulse, my loving husband knelt beside the bedside and earnestly prayed, "Oh, God, spare her life! Remember the boy who used to pray!"

God did hear and restore me. A change of altitude was necessary. Charles transferred back to Chicago, where he spent 10 years in the telegraph office. Those years were so ordinary that one wouldn't dream them to be years that the world notices. Yet the matchless hand of God shaped his chosen vessel during those years. Charles threw his whole heart into his work. Thoroughness was one of the most prominent elements of his character. What he did, he did with all his might. His position as chief of the New York Division required steady nerves and more than ordinary self-control. His first year in Chicago was a great success, and his genial manner won the hearts of hundreds of new acquaintances, from officials to messenger boys.

Chapter 2

A New Affection

Life in the city held many attractions, and one of the most alluring was the Grand Opera. We both loved music and often attended performances there. Fascinating entertainments were taking a firm hold upon us, and we drifted with multitudes in the broad way. But what of Christ's claim upon our hearts? What of the vow Charles had made to God when he prayed for the restoration of my health? Shortly before his Home-going, he attempted to write some of his life story, and though he didn't finish, he did write these lines, which he called "The Backslider's Return."

> First, it is necessary to relate the conversion of my dear wife. Our lives were thrown together providentially from our childhood, and when she was 19 and I was of age, we were married. I had drifted away from God and from my earliest religious training, and after our marriage both of us were thrown into worldly society. We continued there until 1891, when I was transferred because of her illness to the Chicago Telegraph office.

One night shortly before Christmas in 1893, a Christian worker called at our home and invited us to a meeting for children in a neighborhood church. A converted opera singer was to speak and sing. My wife, being interested in music, accepted the invitation. At the service, the noted lady sang:

> There were ninety and nine that safely lay
> > In the shelter of the fold;
> But one was out on the hills away,
> > Far off from the gates of gold.[3]

The song rent her heart from its worldly satisfaction, and she went to the altar with a number of children and gave her heart to Christ. The change that immediately followed was a great surprise to me, for at once she separated herself from the world and testified that she was genuinely converted. She began dealing with me, but I told her that living a Christian life in a telegraph office was an utter impossibility; however, God rewarded her prayers and exhortations with my conversion one month later.

She became a member of Grace Methodist Episcopal Church, which had a membership of 600, mostly people her own age. A revival was in progress, and she begged me to accompany her on a Sunday evening. Reverend Henry Ostrom was the evangelist. While he preached, there arose out of my misty past a vision of the old mourners' bench and revival scenes out in the dear open country; I remembered the blessed experience and

---

[3] Elizabeth Cecilia Clephane, "There Were Ninety and Nine," 1868.

the tender way God had comforted my heart when I was a lad. I thought of those who rose with faces aglow with that wonderful light not seen on sea nor shore and gave their testimonies of a blessed experience. A deep, unutterable yearning to make it my own came into my heart.

Uppermost in my mind was the time when God spared the life of my loved one through my humble prayer, when I promised the Lord that if he would restore her, I would serve him from then on. What of that unfulfilled vow? I could not lift up my head.

My wife had invited me to accompany her to the altar, but I said, "Not tonight" and stoutly refused her. That itself almost broke my heart, for we were rare lovers, and I could readily have laid down my life for her. She left the pew where we were sitting and took her place with the newly converted who stood in one long line at the front. I felt alone without her as a great gulf seemed forever fixed between us, and my heart broke. But I thought of the telegraph office with its associations, the place I occupied, and my future career. A battle raged, and peace tarried. How truly I had reached "the place called Calvary."

A voice seemed to say, "Trust Jesus, surrender to him, and let go," but I had no power to do so. After the service closed, we started home. Being under deep conviction, I could not utter a word but broke out in sobs. We walked 12 blocks, hastily entered our apartment, and without taking time to turn on the lights, we knelt by a chair. There, I poured out my confession to God and asked him to take back the prodigal. My dear wife, but a month-old Christian, did her best to point me to the Savior, and soon the blessed Spirit witnessed with my spirit that the past was all under the blood and that I was his child once more. The wanderer had returned to his Father's house. What joy was mine! Peace flooded into my heart, and I wanted to tell the world that Jesus had saved me. It was like a blissful new wedding day, for now I was able to walk by the side of my loved one, homeward together.

And I shall never forget that hour. The room became glorious with the presence of God. Charles' face was like that of Moses when he came down from the mount; joy and gladness too deep for words filled his heart. In later years, when Charles visited Chicago, he wanted to go at once to visit the spot where Jesus had so wondrously revealed himself to him. The change in him was marked because it was so radical. His first question was that of Paul, "What wilt thou have me to do?" (Acts 9:6). That was his constant inquiry from then on. He made it the *first thing* in his life to be a Christian and felt he must concentrate all his energy upon it.

Immediately, he began witnessing for Christ in the telegraph office. He wanted his fellow workers to enter the enjoyment of a triumph similar to his own. He knew practically nothing about dealing with seekers. His knowledge of the Bible was limited to what he had learned as a child. He read the Scriptures, but where and how to lead a soul to Christ appeared to be one of the most difficult problems. He had no one to guide him and was quite ignorant of the fact that there were books on the subject of personal evangelism that would have been helpful.

He struggled alone – praying, reading, and looking to the Lord to guide and direct him. In later years, Christian workers and Bible students often inquired of him, "How shall we do personal work?"

He would invariably answer them, "Just begin and do it, and let the method unfold by itself."

His first attempt to win a soul is a never-to-be-forgotten one. He went to his office one evening, determined to speak to some of the men that night about their souls' welfare. The operators had been at work at their respective wires for several hours when a lull came, which Charles interpreted as his opportunity. In one corner of the long room sat a man at his desk, apparently with a few spare moments. Back and forth through the length of the room Charles walked before he could summon enough courage to speak to him. Finally, for half an hour he stood beside his desk, engaged in a one-sided conversation. Doubtless, the young man was astonished to find someone talking to him about his soul, for he never made any reply.

Charles left the office feeling downhearted over his first attempt to win a soul. But the following night when he returned home, almost the first words he said were, "Oh, I have something wonderful to tell you! The young man I talked with last night came to me as soon as I entered the office and said, 'I went home last night after our conversation and did just what you told me. It is all settled; I gave myself to Christ.'"

That man was Ernest A. Kilbourne. On that day, the two men began a lifelong friendship and Christian partnership. Their hearts were knit together. Charles had the unique experience of leading his colleague and successor to Christ before he himself had left his native land for Japan, where they would spend their subsequent years working together again, this time toiling for the Lord.

Charles' heart was encouraged through finding this one

soul, so the next night, he was bolder and talked to another telegrapher who had once been an earnest Christian, but who, since coming to the Chicago Telegraph office, had drifted away. Love won Robert Fisher back to God that night. He also had a part to play in the future of The Oriental Missionary Society.

Two had been won for the Lord in less than a week. What encouragement from so little effort! Charles' soul took fire from that very week, and he became a soul winner of the rarest and most original type. In his businesslike manner, he began a systematic effort to win his men, recognizing that men are not saved in bundles but *one by one.*

Charles made opportunities to speak to them about their souls' welfare. He did not wait for a convenient season but prayed and made an advance toward them. He kept a list of several hundred whom he remembered in prayer every day. This was followed by personal effort, and few escaped heart-to-heart talks over the subject that matters most. Such faithful work produced results. His enthusiasm was not one that blazed and then died, but a steady, unabated force that entered into every part of his being.

Men sometimes came to him with questions of conviction or doubts. He would say, "Go home and pray," as there was no place for quiet in an office with hundreds of clicking instruments. He wrote the questions in a notebook, and on his return home, he searched the Bible for hours, often into the early morning, to find a scriptural answer. He learned from practical experience the value of the Word of God, and the following evening his seekers would find an answer to their questions in a word of Scripture. It was God's own Word, and therefore, it could not fail.

In less than six months, he had personally led 75 of his fellow workers to the Lord. All were handpicked fruit. He carried out this personal work in odd moments, as he felt his time belonged to the company. Not once was there the slightest criticism that he neglected business. But he kept an eye open for those moments every night when it was not necessary for the men to be kept steadily at the telegraph key. He learned to use such gaps and capitalized on every minute to sow the seed with full assurance of a harvest. The power of God was behind it. A real revival grew steadily in the office without the aid of a preacher and without a prayer room.

Winning a soul was to Charles what winning a battle is to a soldier, winning a bride to a lover, or winning a race to an athlete. This was his sole passion. His resourcefulness was extraordinary, and none felt that he was simply trying to force religion upon them. As love had made a pathway to the hearts of his fellow workers, they enjoyed having him speak to them, for they knew that their interests were dear to him. Many said, "We felt drawn to him and could tell him everything – the good and the bad – and he would understand."

He had a remarkable ability to enter into the perplexities of his fellow workers. They would come to him with their heart difficulties, and he would seem able to place himself in their particular situations, enter into their feelings, see the difficulty from their standpoint, and then pray to God with them.

One of his operators told him of an overpowering temptation to drink. Instead of reprimanding him, Charles put his arms around him and with tears pleaded to God to destroy his thirst and give him deliverance. Long afterward, that man testified that it was the tears of loving sympathy that won him.

One morning, another fellow worker, who had made a start heavenward some weeks before, came from the office to our home. His breath told the sad story of drink. Charles took him into his study, and the two remained there all day long in prayer. At one point, I heard a snatch of:

Break down every idol, cast out every foe—
Now wash me, and I shall be whiter than snow.[4]

A pause followed, then more prayer, and soon I heard voices singing in unison:

He takes me as I am; He takes me as I am;
He brings His full salvation nigh, and takes me as I am.[5]

There was a sound of praise, and the two men emerged, arm in arm. Their faces were wet with tears. Another prodigal had found a welcome home.

One of his workers lost his 10-month-old baby, and his heart was crushed. This bereaved parent came to his work as usual throughout the child's brief illness, as he needed money to pay the doctor's bills. Charles saw tearstains on the telegraph blanks. Going to the man's side, he quietly slipped his arm around him and said, "I know all about it. I lost a baby sister, and my heart was broken until Jesus came with his healing balm." Another soul was won through that tender sympathy.

Years later, an old associate said of him:

> "Mr. Cowman possessed a certain power over us, and those with the strongest wills bent to his way of thinking without one particle of friction. He made us feel and believe and desire to do what he requested. I could never quite understand this power. As his beaming face looked down upon us at our tables, as those sparkling eyes met ours, every one of us felt that he sought our best, our

---

4   James Nicholson, "Whiter Than Snow," 1872.
5   John Bowring, "In the Cross of Christ," 1825.

highest good, and as we sat there before him, we were permanently changed."

Another wrote:

> He helped us feel that we were stronger and our work better than we had dared to believe. His sunniness brought hope to everyone around him, and his air of distinction was so manifestly an air of purity and not of pride that it helped us keep ourselves separate from what was base and trivial. His great, glorious calmness was the most powerful of all. Things just settled themselves in his presence without as much as a word. He always spoke to us with a soft tone. He never shouted out his orders, and we breathed different air altogether when we were working for him.

Charles had power to transplant his belief, his enthusiasm, and his courage into others. He created a type that reproduced itself. The converts won in the office were infected with his own consuming passion, for they ached for souls too. The work hours kept most of them from attending church, so Charles engaged the parlor of a nearby downtown hotel for an hour on Sunday afternoons, and he began simple services there. Prayer, singing, and reading God's Word were followed by a short exhortation by one of the newly converted. They strengthened each other and soon organized themselves as the Telegraphers' Mission Band.

This band became the foundation of a great missionary society. Once a month, they gave their humble offering of $20 for missions. Charles said to this company, "Why not reach telegraphers in other cities?" He had never been the kind of a man simply to follow in the beaten tracks, but was always ready for new ventures that required courage and faith. And so, he formulated a plan. The men sent letters to telegraph operators all over the United States, Great Britain, and Australia with Gospel tracts explaining the way of salvation, and the results were most encouraging.

For a man with a strong nature such as Charles had, to do things by halves was not possible. Having come boldly out for the Lord, he could not keep from taking up active work in the harvest fields of the world. Personal work, open-air services, Sunday school, and mission work – all engaged his energies.

Charles became deeply interested in the welfare of men who frequented mission halls. One Sunday, he attended a service in a district of Chicago known as Little Hell. The leader, mistaking him for a minister, invited him to preach the following Sunday evening. He accepted the invitation, and during the following week he prepared his first sermon.

He spent hours in prayer and the study of the Word. That Sunday evening, the hall was crowded to its limit with men and women of the worst sort. Some reeled down the aisle in a drunken stupor; others were soon fast asleep. The friendless were there, the homeless, the penniless. As he viewed the crowd of sin-marred faces, Charles set aside his sermon and talked directly to the hearts of that crowd. With tears, he begged them to give up their lives of sin and come to Jesus. And they came weeping, a long altar full. He was there until midnight, praying with them. What a great encouragement he received from his labors in Little Hell, where he spent every Sunday evening after that. In later years, when he went to Japan as a missionary, many of these "down-and-outs" whom he had led to Christ became his faithful supporters.

Abandoned and desperate men felt he was not only a voice, but also a friend. He always hoped for the most hopeless, identified good points in the worst, and sent a man away feeling he was trusted once more, not only by a friend, but also by Christ. I found graphic accounts of some of these people among his papers – soiled old letters, each one of them the confession of a soul, the sob of a broken heart, or the cry of a cold and starving man.

Dr. A.I. Berninger, his physician friend, wrote his recollection of this period:

> Charles opened a mission at 35 North Chicago Avenue. He was a wise fisherman and believed in using bait, which was truly effective in his mission, for he had many converts. The room he rented was a storeroom with a basement that was cleaned up, the walls whitewashed, and a stove put in for heating. The announcement at its opening stated that any man might come and stay all night free in the basement, if he would attend the preaching service upstairs and be orderly. The ones who came early could have their choice of a place below for spreading their newspapers to sleep on. A hired janitor kept the fire at night and maintained order. This was effective bait and gave a respectful hearing. These men knew they could sleep at the police station, but they preferred this place. The result was many conversions.

Little Hell became a training college for service in far wider fields. Thus, early in his Christian life, Charles drank deeply of the Master's spirit; he worked and prayed for the conversion of the most helpless and degraded.

Chapter 3

Another Life Crisis

Charles had lived as a Christian for a year, and among the members of Grace Methodist Episcopal Church, none were more zealous for souls than he. Quite unconsciously, he had become a leader among the young people. An earnest brother, George Simister, was also a soul winner, and he often took Charles aside to tell him of a wonderful blessing that he had received – entire sanctification. But since his second encounter with the Lord, Charles had never lost the thrill of his first love and never waned in glad responsive gratitude to the Lord, so he saw no need of being sanctified. However, something happened at the office one night, and the calm, quiet, self-possessed man became impatient and spoke harshly to one of his men. Quickly he asked the man's forgiveness, but peace left his heart, and he continued in this state of mind for almost a week.

Charles sent for Mr. Simister, who said, "Brother Cowman, you need to have your heart cleansed from all sin." In the simplest manner, he explained that after conversion, "the old man" of sin still remains and the only remedy is cleansing through the blood of Christ.

Charles seized the opportunity. He regarded nothing as

important as having his heart cleansed from all sin, and he began to seek it with full purpose of soul. During this time, he penned these lines:

> "I was profoundly impressed and powerfully sustained, almost absorbed by the Word, 'This is the will of God, even your sanctification' (1 Thessalonians 4:3). 'If any man will do his will, he shall know of the doctrine' (John 7:17). These words cannot be too deeply engraved upon the heart. I will ever seek to have my will one with the will of God."

He was impressed with the words of Drummond:

> What is the end (purpose) of life? The end of life is not to do good, although many of us think so. It is not to win souls, although I once thought so. The end of life is to do the will of God. That may be in the line of winning souls or doing good, or it may not be. If we could have no ambition past the will of God, our lives would be successful. The only great thing in life is what of God's will there is in it. The maximum achievement of any man's life after it is all over is to have done the will of God.

Charles wrote in his notebook, "I have committed myself and my all into God's hands, and he has accepted the offering. Life henceforth can never be the same."

Those who knew him before and after this experience could not question that he had found a new secret of power for his own life and work. He had come into a fresh experience, a second definite work of grace, a crisis as radical as that of regeneration.

He was truly sanctified, and holiness had not only an advocate in him but also an illustration. He began an unbroken walk with God, and it was his lifelong determination to bring others under the power of the same soul-cleansing blood. A penciled note in his Bible read:

God first.

Wife and home second.

Telegraph office third.

The days of small things were now past. From this time forward, he would open his mouth wide that God might fill it. Little by little, he was led out to possess more territory until the Lord could entrust him with the "wealthy place" where he stood with steady nerve and unfaltering faith throughout the years that followed.

Now and then, invitations came from pastors of larger Chicago churches to address their congregations. His messages were seldom more than 20 minutes long, and they took the form of a simple testimony of what God was doing among the telegraphers of his office. Many a man went home from the service with a fresh vision of what he could do for Christ in his own place of business.

A preacher who was noted for his oratory invited him to speak at his Sunday evening service, as he too had heard of the revival in the telegraph office and longed to know the secret of this businessman's success. After the service, he called Charles to his study and said, "I try to win souls but fail every time. Can you tell me the reason?"

The two men were alone. They told the janitor not to disturb them or admit anyone. The tower clock struck three before they walked homeward. They had met Someone during those hours, and the next Sunday, a new man stood at the pulpit with a new heart and a new message. "What has happened to our minister?" the people whispered.

A great revival broke out in that church. One night, this great learned man came down from the pulpit, slipped his arm around Charles, and said, "God bless you, Brother Cowman, for your faithfulness to me that night. I would rather have the love of God shed abroad in my heart and witness the scenes of the past two weeks than to have the world at my feet."

In the weeks that followed, Charles received invitations from many pastors to address their congregations. These he accepted as the voice of the Lord. Relying on him, he ventured forth into this new field, saying, "My preparation must come directly from him upon whom my soul continually feeds."

Thus, without human authority or professional training, this layman became a minister of the Word. And if he who inspires and fulfills the Word orders a man to preach it, who shall dare dispute the ordination or the call? From that time, Charles, without assuming any clerical dignity, continued to preach the Gospel.

Chapter 4

The Volunteer

A national convention of the Epworth League, the youth of the Methodist Episcopal Church, was held in Chattanooga, Tennessee. Charles and I went as delegates from Grace Church. Bishop Isaac W. Joyce had just returned from a world tour, and his soul had been stirred as he had looked upon fields white unto harvest. The thousands who assembled were swayed by his messages. Charles' soul took fire that day. Until this time, he had given little or no thought to the regions beyond. His world was tied up in the telegraph office, his church, and his home. He had never hinted that he would ever see the foreign field, but now he caught a vision.

This was his first missionary awakening, and the plea for the support of national workers strongly appealed to him. He was never influenced by excitement, nor had he been carried away from his position by infectious impulses, but gradually the Holy Spirit gently aroused him, and he received an unconscious preparation for the years ahead.

At this convention, he received a tract on the subject of tithing. He saw its truth, and on New Year's Day, he opened his first account with the Lord. When his monthly salary came, he set aside a tenth of it and entered into his notebook, "The Lord's tithe." From that day to the end of his life, nothing ever came into his hand that was not first of all tithed. He felt the Lord was also interested in the way he spent the remaining nine-tenths, so in his account book was a page for "offerings."

When special needs arose in the church with discussions of bazaars and fairs, Charles usually took the floor and made a ringing speech; he told them that he did not agree with that method of maintaining the house of the Lord and that the scriptural plan was tithing. A "Tithers League" was formed and carried out successfully, so the need for festivals and fairs to raise money disappeared. Best of all, the spiritual life of the church increased.

Later, Charles decided he would give all his income to God, except the amount needed for his actual personal need. He carefully weighed *needs* and *wants*. "How much can we do without each month? Just what do we actually need, and what can we spare for the Lord's work?"

He kept all his accounts for the Lord's inspection and made no investments except those in the work of God. "Lay not up for yourselves treasures upon earth" was impressed upon his mind early in life (Matthew 6:19); in later years, when several inheritances came to him, he did not tithe these but gave them entirely to the Lord. He felt called to a life of self-denial for Christ and missions, and thus God kept him always at a place where heroic exercise of faith was necessary. He resolved that everything that flowed into his life should flow out of it in still greater volume.

We lived in a beautiful, well-furnished home, but we exchanged it for a small apartment in order to support another African worker. People often asked him, "How can you afford to support so many workers?"

He usually replied, "I cannot afford it. I can sacrifice it."

When the call came to leave all and go to Japan, had he not given away all his income, he would have had more than sufficient to support us both. But God had another plan, and to others he entrusted the honor of paying the steamer fare and lending a hand.

In 1894, Moody Church in Chicago hosted a great missionary convention. Dr. A.B. Simpson was the principal speaker. Many missionaries were present from various corners of the world. Charles' heart was strangely moved when Dr. Simpson told of a young businessman who in simple faith had gone to the heart of Africa with his wife and small child, trusting God to supply their needs. Charles had never heard of such an extraordinary course of action, and the self-denial of these servants of God gripped him.

When the offering was taken, he laid his entire monthly salary, together with his beautiful gold watch, on the collection plate. After the offering came the call for volunteers to go out as missionaries. He said to me, "That means you and me, so let us stand and show our colors."

Charles began reading missionary literature about India's millions. He believed that God was calling him to India, but he did not know what step to take to reach this land. I did not feel called to India, and our physician said I could not live in such a climate.

In the providence of God, Charles met Dr. Arthur T. Pierson, who had heard of his work in the telegraph office and his influence with the young people in our church. Dr. Pierson said to him with much emphasis, "Young man, wait for God's hour." Charles sought a word from the Lord. He prayed, waited, watched, and expected; suddenly the word came: "Stay thou there until I bring thee word" (Matthew 2:13). What a mistake Charles would have made if he had gone to India out of the will of God. He forever praised the Lord for the closed-up way.

After this, he purposed that since he was not to be a missionary to India, he would joyfully carry on his work for the Lord in the telegraph office. He did not look back with a sad, lingering look, as if to say, "Why couldn't I have gone to India? I am having God's second best." Rather, his heart overstepped the boundaries of kindred and country to take in the whole world. A world map became a sort of prayer book.

Sensing his lack of Bible knowledge, Charles began a special course offered by Garrett Biblical Institute in Evanston. He worked in the telegraph office from five o'clock until midnight. This schedule gave him opportunity to attend morning classes at Dwight L. Moody's Bible Institute for Home and Foreign Missions. He reveled in the study of God's Word and spent the next six years in diligent Bible study with one objective – to qualify himself for personal soul winning.

In the strictest and most literal sense, Charles believed the Bible to be an inspired book, that it not only *contained* the Word of God, but also *was* the Word of God. It was the food that fed his soul and put iron into his blood. Therefore, every day he sought to get fresh insight into the Scriptures and a direction for the new day.

He followed a unique method of Bible study. He would read through one book of the Bible at a sitting. The next day he would reread it. This was often continued for a week at a time or longer, until he thoroughly mastered the contents. He likened this method to that of a landscape painter who first draws an outline, then adds a tree, a flower, and a brook.

What a thrill of joy he experienced when he found some fresh promise. No excavator for buried gold could have had greater delight than he in the treasures he discovered in the Bible. He secured various translations, but he loved the King James Version best of all.

Charles' library contained good books, including the

commentaries of Matthew Henry, Adam Clark, James Gray, and others. *The Life of Charles G. Finney* and *The Life of David Brainerd* made a deep impression on him. He loved Dr. Arthur T. Pierson's books and Dr. A.M. Hills' book *Holiness and Power*. J.A. Wood's *Perfect Love* and *Purity and Maturity* were among his favorites. One that he read perhaps more than any other was Andrew Murray's *Humility*. He knew this great missionary from South Africa personally because he attended his lectures as a student.

Charles read widely, even while walking in the fresh air. He never allowed fragments of time to go to waste. But he always remembered that the supreme satisfaction for holy service is not intellectual, but spiritual. He tended to describe himself as only a shepherd dog, ready to run after the lost sheep and bring them back to the Shepherd.

Chapter 5

The Call

The Sunday morning service in Grace Methodist Episcopal Church had just begun when a young Japanese man took his seat directly in front of Charles and me. At the close of the service, Charles learned that the visitor, the Reverend Juji Nakada, had come to America to seek help for his preaching, because he said he had "run out of methods." He had become a student at Mr. Moody's Bible Institute, as the evangelist's fame had reached Japan.

Nakada was cordially invited to the Monday evening holiness meetings led by Dr. J.R. Boynton, one of the leading physicians of the city, who had been sanctified wholly a few weeks earlier. Juji Nakada listened for the first time to an old-fashioned holiness sermon.

Dr. A.M. Hills was staying at the institute as a guest. He gave Nakada a book called *Holiness and Power*. Juji sought earnestly to be filled with the Holy Spirit, and it was not long until his hungry heart was satisfied. He soon felt strongly impressed that God would send him back to his people to preach full salvation to them.

The Telegraphers' Mission Band assumed the support of the

Japanese brother and sent him back to his own country rejoicing. He became their representative in Japan and traveled all over the land holding evangelistic services. The Band most eagerly read his reports at their meetings. In this way a missionary fire was kindled that was never extinguished.

There is a double presence of the Lord for the consecrated believer. He is present in the heart and in the events of life. As yet, it had not dawned upon Charles that God had chosen him to be Nakada's coworker and to find his permanent home in Tokyo. But God was leading his child and gently loosening his hands from the work in the telegraph office.

We find on a blank page in Charles' Bible this brief sentence: Called to Japan. August 11, 1900, 10:30 a.m.

"There was no day like that" (Joshua 10:14). It stood alone in the history of his life. From then on, all his life was altered.

It was not in a crowded gathering where there was a great wave of missionary enthusiasm, but it was in the hush of the Sunday morning, away from his busy office, with a heart stilled to hear the smallest whisper of his voice that Charles received the call that bore him through all kinds of tests in the years that followed.

On my return from a church service, he met me with a tear-stained face, took my hand in his, and led me into the study where he broke the wonderful news. He read the verse that clinched his faith: "Go ye also into the vineyard, and whatsoever is right I will give you" (Matthew 20:4). To him this meant everything – a divine commission and a divine supply. The vision was almost blinding.

He had prayed earnestly that I might be willing to accompany him, and the answer was not long delayed. I said, "Charles, six weeks ago while I was all alone, God spoke to me about going to Japan, and I have kept it hidden away within my heart, waiting for the right moment to tell you."

Just at the time when the call was ringing in his heart, he received another splendid offer of a promotion from the telegraph company. His officials had an inkling that he was leaving the telegraph service, so they left no stone unturned to keep this valuable worker with them. But God's clear call had come; a divine voice was calling him. His friends were afraid that if he went to the mission field, he would waste his life and forget that the Master said, "Except a corn of wheat fall into the ground and die, it abideth alone: but if it die, it bringeth forth much fruit" (John 12:24). However, the blessings that followed far outweighed anything of worldly advantage he was laying down. When Charles returned after many years, he said, "I have never had one hour of regret throughout these wonderful years. I would have gone to the ends of the earth alone for the enjoyment of the unspeakable fellowship of Christ."

Like the apostle Paul, Charles was willing to become a fool for Christ's sake, and not a few of his business associates regarded him as such. They only saw his opportunity for enriching his own life. He could not fail to understand the reasons why his officials urged him to remain. At that time, there were also many conversions among his men. But he had a feeling that the hand of God was upon them for something he could scarcely discern.

Charles' work at the telegraph office ended. The time had come. To tarry longer would have been disobedience. God had planned a different field from India for him with a fuller ministry, but the time had not come for it to be revealed. Had he told him all that he had planned for him, it would have staggered him, and he might have drawn back. So he guided him step by step, first calling him out in a small way into a life of faith, then a little larger, until trust was easy. He dared to go where the Holy Spirit led him and to leave the consequences with him. He did not blaze his own path through life; God made it for him.

We had to dispose of our home and furniture. We put an

advertisement in the newspaper and a large sign in the window, but not a person came near. Remembering Gideon's fleece, Charles asked that we might have some sign from the Lord. He took down the "For Sale" sign while he prayed definitely and asked the Lord to direct someone to the house.

Almost immediately, Robert Fisher, his second convert, called and asked what he was going to do with his apartment and furnishings. In less than one hour, everything was in Fisher's possession. This was indeed a confirming of the Word.

Charles was now ready for the fulfillment of the promise, "Every one that hath forsaken houses, or brethren, or sisters, or father, or mother,… for my name's sake, shall receive an hundredfold, and shall inherit everlasting life" (Matthew 19:29).

Mr. Fisher wanted immediate possession, so it was necessary to vacate. Into our home some months before had come a small eight-page paper, *God's Revivalist*, edited by the Reverend Martin Wells Knapp of Cincinnati. The paper had such a deep spiritual tone that Charles longed to meet its editor before we sailed to Japan, so we went to Cincinnati for that purpose.

"How homeless we felt as we walked out of our apartment," Charles said to a friend, "but I look forward to the time when, on the mission field, I shall be literally homeless indeed, as was my Master, for doubtless much of my life will be spent in itinerant and pioneer work, away from the little spot I shall call home."

God's Bible School, College, and Missionary Training Home was in embryo in Cincinnati under Rev. Knapp's direction. Charles had spent six years at the Moody Bible Institute and had some experience in training young people. A warm friendship sprang up between the two men, and we spent six happy weeks in the autumn of 1900 at this new school while we waited for further orders to leave for Japan.

We were on our way under our own church missionary board; a cable had arrived that stated the sailing date. There was a vacancy in one of the mission schools, and Charles was to fill the position as a teacher of English, and I was to be a teacher of music.

During those days a stranger burden possessed Charles' heart. The glow of going turned to gloom, which he could not understand. At such times it was best to be quite still and inquire of the Lord as to its meaning, so for three days, he scarcely ate or slept. God was ordering a halt. Rev. Knapp carried a similar burden.

There was not the slightest doubt about his definite call. The Enemy never touched that, and light soon came that revealed God's plan in the stillness of the early dawn. That particular meeting with God was the turning point of all Charles' future life. The *steps* are ordered, and the *stops* as well. If we take the first step, our obedience will give God a chance to show us the next.

On a December morning, Charles was up early for his quiet time. He wanted to talk the matter over with the Lord and be assured of his will beyond all doubt. As the glorious sunrise stole over the Kentucky hills, he stood in the doorway, his face toward the dawn, his eyes aglow with a holy light. As he looked into my face, I wondered what he was hesitating to tell me. What secret did he hold that had no words for expression? Handing me a New Testament, he simply pointed toward Matthew 20:4 and said, "God has again spoken to me through these words, 'Go ye also into the vineyard, and whatsoever is right I will give you.'" He added, "I am sure that God means for us to launch forth into his work quite apart from any missionary society and trust him for everything. It is his will for us; we must obey."

It was no mere child's play to which God had called his servant, to forego all methods of self-help, cut loose from the old moorings, and launch forth upon the bare Word. But he wrote in his diary on that day, "I made an unreserved, an unconditional, cheerful, and eternal surrender of myself to God. I do not feel the least bit of anxiety about my future path. I want only to be holy."

This seemed to Charles to be the plan: to go forward at God's call and let him supply the need. He plunged gladly into a life of trusting the Lord alone, and he found that God promises his resources to those who undertake the program of God. He simply fell into his place in the divine plan.

The next Sunday morning, he conducted a service in a little church in the suburbs of Cincinnati. At the close, a woman slipped a dollar bill into his hand. Wholly unsolicited, this first dollar, of more than a million and a half that were later entrusted to him for the work in the fields, was received with perhaps the greatest joy of all, for it came as a token that God was indeed the voice that had spoken to his soul the previous week.

At a Christmas convention at the new Bible school, Charles had an opportunity in an afternoon service to tell of his call to Japan. A man sat in the audience with deep conviction. He had traveled a long way to this convention to seek the blessing of a clean heart. He came to the altar, and Charles was quickly by his side. This man had been a Presbyterian elder for 20 years, but during that service, he realized that he had never been born again. Soon, he was rejoicing in the witness of sins forgiven. The next day, he was back at the altar, seeking the blessing of a clean heart, and the Lord again used Charles to lead a soul over into Canaan.

A week after the convention, this man sent a letter with a check for $300. It read, "Please accept this gift for your steamer fare to Japan." He had gone to Iowa, sold a farm, and sent a tenth of the amount he had received, which was just sufficient for the fare. Could anything have been more directly from God's own hand? How marvelously everything opened up when God's hour had arrived!

We soon said goodbye to our new friends in Cincinnati

and were off to Chicago for final farewell meetings. In the meantime, friends had learned of our plan to go to the mission field by trusting in Jesus alone; many were alarmed because we were starting off with nothing behind us *but God*. People of our church objected to such a daring step. They prophesied failure. Some waited to see how the glow of our enthusiasm would endure the strain and toil of learning the language and living by faith. Had we waited for the opinion of everyone, we would have died before the occasion could have improved.

Later, Charles wrote, "If you are willing to run risks for God, he will never fail you. Be sure you are doing his will, then forward march, come what will, and those who waited to see you fail will come and help you after you have made the venture."

In one of the services, a man slipped a check into Charles' hand and said, "Please accept this for the first year's rent of your proposed Bible training school. It does not represent any abundance of wealth, but if you, for Christ's sake, can separate from your business and everything and go without purse or scrip, I cannot give less than this." The check was for $240.

A simple ordination service was held in Chicago in late December 1900. Martin Wells Knapp had accompanied us there. He felt that Charles was answering his own call (as he had felt called some years before). He, the Reverend Seth B. Rees, his son Byron, and the Reverend Charles Stalker laid their hands upon Charles and me, separating us unto the ministry.

Many old friends attended. Among them was Charles' best friend, Ernest A. Kilbourne. How greatly Charles disliked leaving him. But Mr. Kilbourne pledged his prayers and promised to stand back of the Telegraphers' Mission Band that was so dear to him.

In Charles' last message, he spoke of his prospective work with glee, fired by the prospect. This is an excerpt from his message:

Some years ago I read a book entitled *Dawn on the Hills of Tang*. It said, "The investment of life is the most momentous of all human decisions." Later, I read *Investment of Influence*, and this gave me a larger vision that it is not a light thing to live out a whole human life and not live it in such a way as to bring large returns.

As I have pondered over these facts, a great longing has come to me to give our young people this true conception of a life investment – and not to these only but to hundreds of Christian men and women with wrong views of true success. In this commercial age, even the preacher is tempted to leave the pulpit and engage in some work that will bring larger returns in dollars and cents. The paramount question that towers above every other, not only in youth but at whatever point we may have reached, is this: "How can I now invest the rest of my life so it will bring the largest return?"

Later, I found these lines penned in Charles' Bible:

> God is looking for a man or woman whose heart will be always set on him and who will trust him for all he desires to do. God is eager to work more mightily now than he ever has through any soul. The clock of the centuries points to the 11th hour.
>
> The world is waiting yet to see what God can do through a consecrated soul. Not the world alone, but God Himself is waiting for one, who will be more fully devoted to Him than any who have ever lived; who will be willing to be nothing that Christ

may be all; who will grasp God's own purposes; and taking His humility and His faith, His love and His power, will, without hindering, continue to let God do exploits. There is no limit to what God can do with a man, providing he does not touch the glory.

Late in December came the final parting from Chicago. We turned our faces westward.

Chapter 6

Launching Forth

> The tender light of home behind,
> Dark heathen gloom before,
> The servants of the Lord go forth
> To many a foreign shore:
> But the true light that cannot pale
> Streams on them from above,
> A light divine, that shall not fail—
> The smile of Him they love.[6]

On the morning of February 1, 1901, a little group of friends, among them a number of telegraph operators, stood on the pier at San Francisco to wave farewell to us. At noon, the gangplank was lifted, the steamer slowly moved away from the dock, and the SS *China* began to plow her way across the Pacific. It was an hour not of sadness but of triumph.

Our fellow travelers who saw Charles walking the deck day after day doubtless mistook him for a businessman going abroad for his company. He kept to himself and spent a great deal of time in prayer. One of the travelers said of him, "There

---

6   Sarah G. Stock, from Church Missionary Hymn Book, 1898.

seems to be something on that man's mind." Yes, there was something, and that something was lost souls and his responsibility to his Master.

A storm at sea was a thrilling experience with the waves in a heroic mood engaged in pitched battle, awful but ravishing. The storm caused a delay of three days.

Many nights we stood for hours together and listened to the music of the waves, then reluctantly said good night to the sea and stepped into our cabin to be rocked in the cradle of the deep. We did not feel alone, but as if invisible armies filled the air. We expected great and mighty things.

On February 21, we saw the dim outline of a shore, our first glimpse of a foreign land. This was a great day. Amid a chattering crowd, we went ashore. Juji Nakada was there to greet us. It seemed like a homecoming.

We now were face to face with the teeming multitude. Charles felt a great aloneness at first; he felt the power of the spiritual force against which his life was hurled. The fiends of darkness seemed to sit in sullen repose on that land. The battle was set; the hour had come. The task was not romantic but one that could exhaust the resources of the best.

The first entry in his notebook upon arrival was this:

> "Tokyo, Japan, February 22. A new era in our lives. New responsibilities, new hopes, new avenues of thought, new subjects for prayer. Oh, for faith, unyielding faith! My soul yearns for a close alliance with God."

During his first month, Charles saw at once the utter impossibility of evangelizing the Orient by Western agencies alone. Devoted Japanese would have to carry out the work. Only they could move the hearts of their own people. He witnessed the effectiveness of Juji Nakada's preaching. The foreigner's voice possesses a tone that falls cold and heavy, but a countryman's voice pleasantly touches the heart. Knowing the sentiments, traditions, and trains of thought among the people, the indigenous ones can strike home with illustrations and imagery in ways quite unknown to the foreign missionary.

The pattern that God gave Charles meant an utter obliteration of self. He was not seen as a leader, but rather was found hidden away while the Japanese Christians came to the front. He delighted in developing the efficient powers of other men and preferred to be in the background. For one as intense as he was, the ability to lower himself and his own interest was little less than marvelous.

Charles and Nakada dreamed of a great Bible training institute where hundreds of Japanese workers might be trained. But with no denominational board nor human resources to back them, it looked like a mere dream indeed. They could understand well the feelings of Nehemiah's little company in their attempt to rebuild the walls of Jerusalem when the mockers jeered, "What do these feeble Jews?" (Nehemiah 4:2). But God often accomplishes his work with the weakest instruments.

At that time, there was no distinctive Bible training institute in Japan and no Holiness Movement. These pioneers would have to blaze a new trail. The aim of the institute would not be to produce classical scholars, but young men and women who could handle their mother tongue with effect, who were steeped in the Bible, and who could proclaim it well enough to arrest and influence all classes of people.

A diligent search was immediately made for a suitable building in which to begin. In his notebook Charles wrote:

April 2, 1901

Today we have been taught a lesson on *exactly timed guidance*. Brother Nakada and I called upon the landlord of the Jimbo-cho mission property. We were delayed in getting through the crowded streets, but reached the house about 9:30 and found a pleasant Japanese man, about 50 years of age. We made known to him our errand, and he smilingly said, "I have wished to rent my buildings to Christians as I have found them so reliable and prompt in paying their bills." It was not long before we possessed the lease for the building. The rental was but a trifle more than $240.

As we left, a gentleman rode up in a jinricksha with the express purpose of renting the building, but he was 10 minutes too late. I could only stand in awe before the King of Kings, who hears and answers prayer. There can be but one reason for this: *God* is in it. How blessed to have God as your partner!

How wonderfully God led, even in the smallest details. The building was singularly suited to the need. It was right in the heart of that city of three million souls. The first floor had room for a good-sized mission hall as well as an apartment for Brother Nakada. On the second floor were rooms for prospective students and for us as well. We quickly put it in order and hung a large sign over the entrance that read:

Jesus Doctrine Mission Hall

Services Every Night, Everybody Welcome

Scarcely had the signboard been placed when a scholarly looking gentleman called to inquire about the meaning of it. M. Takamaye was an educated man and was always searching, like the Athenians, for something new. This was his first direct contact with Christians. We gave him a New Testament to read, and every evening for a week he faithfully came to the services. Soon he was rejoicing as a child of God.

The mission hall had been open less than a week when not enough personal workers could be found to deal with the many seekers after one rousing evening service. Brother Nakada beckoned to Charles to go to the front, as one young seeker could speak a little English.

One of the greatest trials of a new missionary is the inability to speak the language. To Charles, eager to win souls, this was a tremendous test, but the Lord took pity on him and allowed a "handful of purpose" to fall across his path.

He went quickly to the altar and took the young man aside. For more than an hour, they had what the young man afterward termed "the most delightful conversation of my lifetime," for he learned that there was a God of love – a God who loved him.

It was customary to take the name and address of each seeker. This young man gave his: S. Taniguchi, Central Telegraph Office, Tokyo. Charles' joy was unbounded. This was the *first soul* God had permitted him to lead to Christ in Japan, and he was a telegraph operator!

The next evening, Taniguchi brought two other young telegraph operators. They too could converse in English. Before the week ended, seven young telegraph operators had been gloriously converted. They became an evangelizing force in the greatest telegraph office of the Far East. The adversary must have trembled.

They were immediately set to reading the Word of God, and

a Telegraphers' Mission Band was formed to reach others, an exact replica of the Chicago band. S. Taniguchi was its leader.

Was it too early to put such responsibility on him? Charles promised to teach him the Scripture. Every evening, he was ready, carrying his Bible and notebook wrapped up in a large blue handkerchief. He walked five miles after working all day in the office. It was pouring rain one night, but he rapped at the door and stood there, dripping wet. When questioned why he did not take a jinricksha, he hung his head and made no reply. Several nights later, we understood. Though his monthly salary was only $7, he had a few spare cents left over after paying for his lodging. But he spent these on New Testaments, which he gave away to other workers in his office.

After a few weeks, God sent him throughout the empire as an evangelist. He had a consuming passion for souls and saw men seeking God everywhere. He lived only three more years and burned out for God.

One night, while passing through a very narrow street, someone from our group shouted out through the megaphone, "A Jesus doctrine meeting will be held tonight at the mission hall in Jimbo-cho. Anyone desiring peace, come and hear about the true God."

In a little out-of-the-way home sat an elderly couple, and the message reached them. "Anyone desiring peace." It was like sweet music, and the old grandmother thought, "Peace! What a lovely word, but *where* can it be found? Can it be possible that, after all our weary years of searching, at last we shall find peace? Perhaps these foreigners can tell us. I will go."

The little woman was the first arrival of the evening. She was bent with age and hobbled along with a cane. She sat on the front seat and listened raptly. At the close of the service, we learned something of her life story. Sixty years before, she had married a fine young man. When they started life together, they decided they would lead righteous lives. As the priests were their religious leaders, naturally they consulted them and became faithful attendants at the temple. They observed every festival and devoutly worshiped each idol. But as the years went on, they still had the same heart yearnings that were never satisfied.

The priest told them that if they would visit the various temples of the land, they might find peace. They had considerable money and did not need to work for their living, so they started on their quest. They became pilgrims, devoting their lives to religion. Year after year, they visited temples and tramped hundreds of miles, often far up on a mountain where a dumb idol stood. Hours of hard climbing took them to some shrine where they received written prayers from the priest in charge. But they always returned with the same dull ache in their hearts. Still, they continued their search for 60 long years.

Their money was now all spent, and they were too old for traveling. They had to come to Tokyo and settle down in a tiny room to wait until the end.

The aged woman came every night for two weeks. But one night the old despairing look had vanished, and in her face was a heavenly light as she said, "I have found peace. I have found Jesus."

She brought her husband. Over the pulpit hung a banner with Matthew 11:28: "Come unto me, all ye that labour and are heavy laden, and I will give you rest." The old man was fairly entranced. Tears began to trickle over his wrinkled cheeks. Pointing to the banner, he said, "I never heard such gracious words as these." He too was converted, and this couple, whom we named "Grown Old Waiting," became a continual inspiration to us. They were just two of many who had groped for long years in darkness.

During the first month, 90 souls knelt for salvation at the humble altar. Some of the most difficult individuals that were converted were noted idolaters, drunkards, gamblers, the lowest of the low, as well as some in the upper classes. They went back to former associates with glowing faces and vital testimonies.

Charles wrote to a close friend at home:

> We are absolutely free here to pour out our lives to the very last drop. We meet hundreds daily who have never heard the precious Name. It is our great joy to see from among these needy souls large numbers genuinely born again. If only you could have been with us in our service last night. The altar was crowded with earnest seekers. Every seat was occupied – even the window spaces. Nakada San preached, and he is a master of crowds. I was so impressed with one of the seekers right here among these stoical, undemonstrative people. He prayed until perspiration dropped from his face like rain. He struggled toward the light, and we just left him to wrestle it out alone. Finally, someone began to sing, "Nothing in my hand I bring, simply to Thy cross I cling."[7] The light broke through, and he leaped to his feet, praising God with a loud voice. The haunting fear, the self-torture was gone, and he was jubilant in the peace and comfort of simple faith in Christ.

At the opening services, we had prayed for a great ingathering of souls, and that prayer was answered to the full. God alone has the record of the many thousands who were converted on that spot.

We also held open-air meetings. Charles wrote of one of these:

---

7   Augustus Toplady, "Rock of Ages," 1775.

> A number of our students accompanied me yesterday, and I had the privilege of preaching through an interpreter at a great open-air meeting in Uyeno Park. It was not a congregation, nor an assembly, nor a crowd, but a tremendous torrent of human beings, produced by the conflux from 20 points on the compass of this great city. It would have been impossible to preach if some of our students hadn't carried off part of the crowd to another place.
>
> We began at 2:30 p.m. and kept right on for hours. I spoke until my soul and body were nearly bidding each other a final farewell. The spirit of glory rested upon all; I felt there were multitudes who will never, never worship idols again.

To a former telegrapher, a member of the Chicago band, he wrote:

> We are in the midst of an old-fashioned revival and that right here in Japan. Our own small halls would not hold the crowds. We took a step of faith and rented one of Tokyo's largest halls, right down in the very heart of the teeming populace. The doors had scarcely opened when 1,500 people rushed in. Never before have I witnessed such meetings. Great conviction of sin is upon the people; unbelievers are seeking forgiveness; lukewarm professors are being revived. Tokyo is being moved by the power of the Holy Spirit.
>
> It is a solemn work to stand here between the living and the dead. I have never been sorry that God called me to be a missionary, but what an account I shall have to render! The work is glorious and

far exceeds anything I have ever witnessed in America.

God has given us some rare opportunities for witnessing for him. Every Sunday evening, we hold a service right under the very dome of an old pagoda. It is in the courtyard of one of the largest temples in Tokyo, and tens of thousands of worshipers from every corner of the empire assemble here. Just imagine the hour of sunset, the old priests in their temples, burning incense to the idols, their doleful chants, the tolling of bells in a minor tone, and contrast it with a Gospel service at the entrance. One of our students played the cornet last night, and we experienced a real heart-thrill when we heard the clear notes of "Precious Name, Oh, How Sweet." The Christians of our party joined in and sang a verse through; then we sang it in English, and the echo rang through the city and over the hills and vales. Somehow, it seemed to echo all over the Orient. There is a time coming, thank God, if we do our utmost, when his Name shall be made known.

A number of young men and women had already heard the call of God to preach to their own people. Scarcely had the Bible school opened when numbers of applications were received. Charles was overwhelmed. We received as many students as we could accommodate. These earnest ones studied during the morning, held street meetings in the afternoon, and attended the mission hall services in the evening. The object of the school was to make *experiential* preachers. These became great soul winners.

To a questioning teacher of a missionary study class, Charles wrote:

> If we get the idea that people are going to be converted by some educational process instead of the regenerative process, it will be a profound mistake. In these lands are ancient systems of philosophy, religion, and culture; we do not seek to add to these. One thing is lacking: the knowledge of Christ and his salvation. Christ alone is the paramount need.
>
> The early missionaries in Greenland assumed they had to spend a long time in preliminary teaching, preparing the natives to understand the Gospel, so they taught them the principles of the Old Testament, the law of God, and so on without spiritual fruit. One day, when the missionary read the third chapter of John, an old chief was overwhelmed with wonder and joy, and immediately he and many of his people gladly accepted the Savior.
>
> Talk theory to unbelievers, and they are unmoved; tell them merely of blessings in store for their future, and they are often too skeptical or too occupied with the pressure of present necessity to hear what you have to say. But, as experience proves, tell your audience that you have an infallible help for every gambler and every drunkard; proclaim a Savior who has never failed to save immediately every soul that trusted him, both

from the power of sin and its eternal consequences. Then you will soon see that the Gospel is good news to your hearers and that it can command attention and will accomplish the mightiest change the mind can conceive or the heart can desire.

Unbelievers are fast losing faith in the ashes of their fathers and the temples of their gods. The call to grand achievements still increases. Alas! How many are putting their best energies into superficial reform instead of grasping the will of God as revealed in the Word and illustrated in the career of Jesus? I would not have come here to engage in teaching school; there are others who would. Neither would I come to engage in a profession; there are those who would. I would not come for business; there are others who would. But I would come here among these hungry multitudes and live, labor, endure, and die to declare that –

> There is a fountain filled with blood
>   Drawn from Emmanuel's veins;
> And sinners plunged beneath that flood
>   Lose all their guilty stains.[8]

We established our first missionary home in the Jimbo-cho district in the heart of Tokyo. The street was about eight feet wide, lined with markets of every description. European houses in more healthful districts were available, but the high rents made them an impossibility. So we used rooms on the upper floor of the school building. Few westerners would have considered living there, but to Charles, this was just as he had pictured

---

8   William Cowper, "There Is a Fountain Filled with Blood," 1772.

missionary life. He was as happy as if he had been in a palace, for he had no ease-loving spirit.

How friendly the people of the neighborhood were. It was a novelty for them to have missionaries living in their small, narrow street. The strangeness soon melted away, and they smiled at us and even brought food from their homes. They made us welcome. They understood that we had come to do them good.

Deep peace can make us independent of our surroundings and conditions. In a letter home, Charles wrote:

> I wish you could see us in our new home in the Orient! The building that we rented had been used as a children's school, and the tots had taken their *fude* (brushes used for pens) and painted Chinese characters all over the walls. It was a sight to behold and would have made an interesting study for some interior decorator. There was nothing left to do but paint it. I searched through every shop in the neighborhood for paint, but could find nothing but red – a bright red. Now imagine your sitting room, bedroom, and kitchen walls in flaming red! But it is cozy and clean, and that means much out here.
>
> We were able to furnish our home for about $20. Extravagance! I used the $10 gold piece you gave me for that purpose. In our front room, we have straw matting on the floor, a plain couch without springs, two straight-back chairs, and a bamboo center table. The Bilhorn organ given to us by our Grace Church friends fills a space in one corner.
>
> This way, please, to the bedroom, and be careful that you do not fall on the newly painted floor.

Where is the bed? In the corner on the floor. We searched through every secondhand store for a bed but could find none, so we did the next best thing. We made a mattress of bamboo leaves, and there we sleep from midnight until dawn. No dozing after that, as the people are up bright and early in this wide-awake land, and the daybreak sounds are not the singing of birds but the clank of wooden doors opening and closing. It is the best hour for prayer, study of the Word, and the language.

And what about the kitchen? We found a small secondhand stove, which cost the sum of $4. The cooking utensils cost a trifle over $2. In one corner, closed off by a tall screen, is our dining room. For 50 cents we bought some of the quaintest dishes on which were painted pictures of Mount Fuji. Drop in for a day, and such fare as we have we shall give thee. It is usually rice for breakfast, rice for dinner, rice for supper, with no trimmings of milk or sugar.

I do not fancy you would enjoy spending the night with us, as rats, small and large, turn handsprings over our bed. For a change, they hold high carnival, racing around the room and over the ceiling until frightened away.

We feel rich, and thank God every day for permitting us to be here. The center of God's will is our home. Why should we want any other? After all, the words of Jesus are true: "A man's life consisteth not in the abundance of things which he possesseth" (Luke 12:15). We are just as poor as the Lord and his apostles, though we cannot say as he did – that he had no place to lay his head.

That was the spirit that always characterized Charles. The will of God, whatever it might be, was always precious. He never shrank back from hardships. He was a disciple who had literally "left all to follow his Master" and whose consistent walk had illustrated the practical meaning of that little-understood phrase throughout many years. His whole soul was engrossed in his work. No sacrifice, however great, could have turned him aside from his delightful task. It was an enthusiasm with him.

Charles often carried about in his pocket a small volume of *The Life of David Brainerd*, with these words heavily underlined: "I cared not where or how I lived, or what hardships I went through, so that I could but gain souls to Christ. When I was asleep, I dreamed of these things, and when I waked, the first thing I thought of was this great work."

During those pioneer days some amusing incidents occurred. The end of a month had come, and the bills had been paid. Charles strictly adhered to the rule of his life never to incur debt. After the actual need of the Society had been supplied, there was just 10 cents left in his purse. He had provided first for all the others. Little did students guess what a test of faith their missionary was often called to pass through. The last bit of flour had been used the day before, as well as the last bit of butter. The larder was absolutely empty except for half a loaf of bread and a little tea.

A fastidious guest called unexpectedly and remained for supper. I covered the table as usual with a dainty white cloth, and on it, I placed the bread and cups of tea. With as much dignity as if he had been presiding at a banquet, Charles sat at the head of the table with the guest seated at his right. He bowed his head and thanked God for the food, making no apology whatever for the meager serving. We wondered what ran through the mind of our fellow missionary, a well-known author from the British Isles.

Years later, a friend, hearing of this incident, asked with tears, "What did you do?"

Charles replied, "There was nothing to do but pray, 'Give us this day our daily bread.' This we did with all the earnestness we could command."

Many and varied trials during those formative years could have broken the strongest personality, but those who saw Charles day by day saw only smiles and sunshine. He disguised the secret cross he was compelled to carry. To say he escaped suffering would not be true, for there is no keener pain than spirit pain, but God held him in a place of perfect calm. A worker once remarked, "Nothing impressed me more than Brother Cowman's quiet spirit. I never saw him ruffled or upset, although at times I saw him wounded until the tears silently fell over his cheeks. He was a tender, sensitive spirit, but his secret cross became his crown."

Again and again, the Lord put to the test the principle on which we had stepped out in 1901. In many ways the intensity grew. After all, for two people without a family to take a risk of this kind does not seem very striking. But now with a family numbering hundreds, the situation became much more complicated from the human standpoint.

Because we went out with no mission board to back us, we were termed "faith missionaries." Many persons expected to witness a grand failure with our sudden exit when our supplies became exhausted, but they were disappointed. "How long do you expect to remain on the field and carry out the work?" was a question frequently asked of Charles.

"Until the Lord forgets to supply the need," was his unfailing reply. But the Lord never forgot.

Let no one imagine that the only difficulties were financial. These were the least of all. Out where the fight is strong and souls are being delivered, the Enemy often comes in like a mighty flood. Once, during a terrible battle with the Prince of Darkness, another missionary remarked, "What a pity that on top of all these difficulties you have to pray in the funds." But Charles felt that daily trusting for financial needs was one of the strongest blessings.

Often in his Bible and notebook appear memorable covenants in which he consecrated himself anew to God's service and implored fresh gifts of divine grace and power that he might more effectively perform the work which he felt God had called him to do. Beside the verse "No man, having put his hand to the plough, and looking back, is fit for the kingdom of God" (Luke 9:62), he wrote, "He must not even glance back." He noted that Jesus sacrificed six things: personal comfort, social enjoyments, human relationships, worldly ambitions, earthly riches, and physical life.

He wrote once:

> We thank God for every black trial we have ever met, for every onslaught of the archenemy, for through these pressures we have learned to know God and have gained our greatest victories. Often, we have been driven into a corner where it was "go under or go through," but God caused the great waves to become ships which launched us further on and on in things divine.
>
> May we say it for the encouragement of some struggling Christian worker, someone in a hard place today: We have never undertaken a work for the Lord under his direct guidance for the

liberation of precious souls that Satan has not fought us inch by inch. But in the midst of the battle, as we have gone along with God, our spirits have been hushed, and a sweet, still voice has whispered to our inmost hearts, "I am on board; there is no wind wild enough, no storm fierce enough to wreck the vessel which carries the Lord of the earth and sky. Sail on, sail on!"

How full were those days. A few stray lines from his diary read:

"Today is the anniversary of our happy marriage. For weeks we had looked forward to this day, planning to spend it together. But breakfast was scarcely over when three of the workers came in from their country stations with loads of difficulties. In the afternoon, we were summoned in haste to the printing house in Yokohama. We did not return until dark. However, at ten o'clock, wife and I went out for a moonlight stroll and lived over again June 8, 1889."

Another entry read:

"I feel very weary. It was long after midnight before I could retire. The new converts wished to sit up and talk, and it would have appeared very rude to them had I left them. At two o'clock I finally crept into bed, but when the morning dawned, a delegation of Christians was outside my door waiting for further conversation."

Several outstanding visitors came on one occasion from the

north. They had heard that an aggressive missionary was at work in Tokyo. One of them, a young woman from a well-known American college, boldly asked, "Where are your diplomas, your credentials, Mr. Cowman?"

He told her that his college of missions had been the telegraph office in Chicago, and his credentials were found in 2 Corinthians 6:4–10. In her face was a look of amazement, but how little did she realize that a new force had appeared, who, like every leader, was a decade or two ahead of his time, one who was definitely called by God to do a marvelous work.

In later years, after the toil of battle, after the tears, the heartaches, the hardship, the weariness, and the loneliness came the glow and glory, but he would say, "Forbid it, Lord, that I should boast, save in the death of Christ my Lord."[9] A college gave Charles an honorary degree, but he never let it be known. He tucked the parchment away in a drawer of his desk, as he preferred his own title, "Charles E. Cowman, missionary."

On April 2, 1902, Charles wrote:

> My heart is too full for words. This is the first anniversary of our Gospel Mission, and the report which was handed to me reads: "During the year 1901, every night, without exception, we have seen souls coming to Christ; sometimes 1, often 5 and 10; and not infrequently on Sabbath evenings, there have been 20 or more seekers." May our hearts bow down before him in praise for the past and in glad expectancy for the future. The response to the Gospel message has been so profound, so striking. What marvelous results from our slightest efforts! What privilege! But opportunity spells responsibility.

---

9   Isaac Watts, "When I Survey the Wondrous Cross," 1707.

Although the work grew rapidly, it was not a mushroom growth. We dealt with all seekers personally and led them to give up idolatry; hundreds were genuinely born again. Not quantity but quality was the object, but God gave both.

The following excerpts from the yearly report for 1902 show the progress made in the work:

> January 14: Crowds attended the holiness meeting today. No standing room left. The sense of the Spirit's presence was so vivid it was almost visible.
>
> February 12: A packed hall this afternoon. Many went away, unable to get in. I am daily asking God to give us a larger hall for meetings.
>
> April 21: Received a letter today from a poor woman who said that the Lord had impressed her to send $5. She quoted the words of Isaiah 54:2: "Enlarge the place of thy tent." It sent me to my knees, and I claimed from God a larger building.
>
> May 30: We received a gift of $1,000 today. It will be used for purchasing a larger hall. The gift came from an entire stranger. A sentence in his letter read, "I am sure the Lord will give you all that you need."
>
> June 15: Searched for locations, but found nothing suitable. "Thine ears shall hear a word behind thee, saying, This is the way, walk ye in it" (Isaiah 30:21).
>
> July 21: We moved into our new mission hall on Awaji-cho. We had received every dollar needed for its purchase. Yesterday we held an all-day service, and the new hall was crowded. Twenty-seven

> seekers knelt at the altar. We are a united, little band, happy in the Lord, well assured that in his own time "a little one shall become a thousand" (Isaiah 60:22). We know that we are preaching the truth, so we wait upon the Lord.

This mission hall became one of the most strategic centers in Tokyo at that time. Services there continued every night for 10 years, an unbroken record, with 15,000 souls seeking Christ.

We experienced God's providential care several times when great fires swept the city and entire districts were literally in ashes. Once, a fire swept along for more than a mile until it reached the corner where Central Mission Hall was located. The people said, "The next place to burn will be the Jesus Doctrine Building." However, a sudden gust of wind turned the course of the fire, and the flames were not allowed so much as to touch that spot. There it stood, a lone building in the midst of the debris, a silent witness to God's protecting care.

Charles was already feeling the responsibility of leadership in a mission that had grown far beyond his expectation in less than two years. He realized his great need of a fellow worker, and he looked to God for the provision of this need. While he waited in patience and faith, God was raising up an instrument through whom he could work. Often, he is working for us when we least expect it, so when the time of unfolding comes, we receive a sweet surprise that he loves to prepare and bestow upon his waiting children. The helper that God sent was none other than Ernest A. Kilbourne, a helper and true burden bearer.

It was a happy day when the steamer arrived in Yokohama with Brother Kilbourne and his family. Interestingly enough, this was the first person Charles had led to Christ. If he had searched the whole world for one who would be a real fellow worker, another just like him could not have been found. Their lives were the exact counterparts of each other. They moved together in unison. They had the same burning love for Christ, the same compassion for the perishing. They moved along with the same mindset for a quarter of a century without a break in their unity of service.

Friends in the homeland were now beginning to take a lively interest in the mission, and we sent monthly reports to them. In November 1902, we began a small monthly periodical that contained reports of the meetings. Its columns glowed with missionary news. It grew from 6 to 8 pages, then to 10, and afterward to 16. It had but one message: the evangelization of the Orient. Neither Charles nor Ernest had experience as editors, but God gave them gifts to enable them to write what they had seen. The periodical was named *Electric Messages* and was later changed to *The Oriental Missionary Standard* (now called *OMS Outreach*).

The little paper was received with much interest. A fellow telegrapher, Fannie E. Ham, wrote her recollection of it:

> "While working in a testing station for the Postal Telegraph Cable Company in 1904, I received a sample copy of *Electric Messages*. I read it with eagerness and immediately forwarded my subscription. It was published by telegraphers and was full of little telegraphic touches. I had never known a missionary to 'evolve' from a telegraph operator.
>
> "Such development was interesting, and I cut a plug into a spare wire to represent the new prayer line to Tokyo. That old switchboard was long ago discarded, but communication with Japan has never ceased and the invisible current still flows on."

The burden upon the heart of Charles Cowman was to make known that souls without Christ are lost and that we are debtors. It continued to the end of his life. Ernest Kilbourne, his partner, shared this burden with him. The names *Cowman* and *Kilbourne* flowed together and will probably be connected in Jerusalem the Golden. Side by side, they had labored in the telegraph office. Side by side, they toiled under Oriental suns to bring the lost home. Side by side, they lie now in beautiful Hollywood.

Chapter 7

Evangelistic Tours

We had been in Japan less than a year and a half when Charles began evangelistic tours that occupied much of the rest of his life. Three Japanese evangelists and seven students composed the first team. They held services every day and evening, and about 700 souls sought Christ in less than six weeks. Doors suddenly opened everywhere with entire towns and villages having an opportunity to hear the Gospel. Charles wrote:

> Oh, the luxury of roughing it! Tonight, four of us are lodged in a room about 6 feet by 12 feet. The *tatami* (mats) look nice and clean, and the innkeeper is most cordial. He apologized greatly that he had no larger room, but I think that we four can lie down anyway, and that will mean a whole lot after the 10-mile walk in the hot sun. We passed through 14 wholly untouched villages today and preached in the streets while the people listened eagerly. Six splendid high school students asked for New Testaments, saying they had given up

idol worship and had nothing to take its place. We pointed them to the Lamb of God, gave them Scriptures, told them where to begin reading the Word, and prayed with them. They accompanied us to the next village, and as we walked along the roadway, they opened their hearts to us.

We passed through a village where a lad had been brightly converted. He gathered his neighbors into his home, and so many came that the floor broke through, but he did not seem disturbed by it. They carried mats out into the yard, where for two hours the people sat quite still and listened as if their very lives depended on it. Two elderly grandmothers, toothless and slightly deaf, asked us to pray with them because they wished to go to "the country of peace" when their earthly life was ended. Oh, how the need of this land grips my heart!

This kind of work brings us into close contact with the tremendous powers of darkness; however, the kingdom of the devil is under the power of our heavenly Father and only affords means by which his perfect will and counsel can be unfolded. This field is a real battleground, but it belongs to Jesus. Satan disputes the title, contends for every inch of ground, and fights hard to cause a retreat. But "Fight on, my soul, till death!"[10] We have had Japan's hundreds brought to Christ; we must have her thousands. The light is burning through the dense darkness and "Jesus shall reign where'er the sun!"[11]

---

10 George Heath, "My Soul, Be on Thy Guard," 1781.
11 Isaac Watts, "Jesus Shall Reign Where'er the Sun," 1719.

A few days later, he wrote:

> This has been a happy day. We began services this morning about 7:00. Many who heard for the first time last night came early, thinking we were leaving today. It is wonderful to reach people who have never heard the Gospel before. In this spot, we have a parish of over 1 million souls. As we have walked through the country day after day, meeting hundreds and thousands who have never heard one word of the Gospel, my heart has been stirred to its very depth, and by the help and grace of God, *they shall hear*, if it costs every drop of my life's blood. Here am I, Lord; send me (Isaiah 6:8).
>
> If our friends at home could only see the ripe opportunity, so dead ripe, how they would stand back of us and help us to evangelize these millions. "We want to find God. You won't leave us, will you, until we truly find him?" said a dear elderly man with a bent form and whitened hair.

And to a prayer partner, Charles wrote:

> Two splendid young men came to me at the close of a service and said that they felt a real call to preach the Gospel. Both are high school graduates, with bright, keen minds. One is employed in a bank, the other in a silk store. I felt impressed to tell them to come straight to the Bible school, but they will need to be supported because they will have to give up their positions. What an investment for

someone, and what a small sum to support their training ... $90.

Calls are coming from other provinces and other districts, "Give us a church or a small hall where we can worship the true God." A delegate from a large cluster of villages pled with us, "Send us a preacher. If you do not have one with long experience, send someone who can read the Bible and pray and lead us to know God."

How was Charles to turn a deaf ear to such heart cries for help? As usual, he turned to God in prayer and reminded him that he had sent him to the Orient to do his work without purse or scrip. Definite requests were made, plans were well laid, and God never failed him.

These trips inland, joyful as they were, invariably ended in some severe illness. Upon his return from one such trip, Charles was stricken with severe pleurisy; he suffered agony for a number of days and nights. When barely able to be out of bed, he was at work again. He noted in his diary:

> "Confined to the house, but made a missionary map. Looking back on last year, a great advance has been made. We have opened new stations in Japan and Korea. Prayed much for the opening of China. Today have translators at work on the marked New Testament. Meditated on the Word: Matthew 28:17, 'But some doubted.'"

Several times on trips, Charles' life was miraculously preserved. Accompanied by several workers, he visited a great untouched district in the north. He had gone with the purpose of opening a mission station and doing evangelistic work, but on the night of their arrival, a great cyclone struck the town and completely demolished parts of it. The door of the hotel was wrenched from its groove and hurled against him. The next morning, he saw a great tree that had fallen across the entrance to one of the largest temples. The elderly priest was sitting on it with a woebegone expression, a picture of hopelessness and despair. The gods in the temples had been thrown from their shelves, and the people were saying, "If they cannot protect themselves, how can they protect us?"

How splendid does pioneer work sound! In the very word, there is glamor and glow; in the life itself, there is nothing of the kind. An early missionary wrote, "Evangelization of unbelievers is certainly not as thrilling as a romance; it is a desperate struggle with the Prince of Darkness and with everything his rage can stir up in the shape of obstacles, vexations, oppositions, and hatred, whether by circumstances or by the hand of man. *It is a serious task.* Oh, it should mean a life of consecration and faith."[12]

On the first inland trip, they opened several stations. During the next 20 years, they opened 160 interior stations and an equal number of itineration points. Trained Japanese carried on the work, and many became entirely self-supporting.

A letter home described this first inland trip:

> It has been our privilege to visit Brother and Sister Shimidzu, who opened our first station. A party of seven left Tokyo last Monday and traveled all day, reaching a large city near the mountains before nightfall. We stopped overnight and boarded another train at 4:00 in the morning, which carried us farther into the mountains. What an interesting

---

12 Reverend François Coillard of the Zambezi

journey! We traveled in a third-class compartment, and often the atmosphere was blue, as both men and women indulged in smoking. Our fellow travelers were very friendly. We had a splendid opportunity for witnessing to them, and we gave out tracts and preached in the train throughout the entire day. All seemed eager to listen.

When descending from the train, one of our party suggested that as it was still twilight, we hold a street meeting. So after supper at an inn, we all went out and preached on various street corners. People flocked like doves to the windows, and we had great liberty to tell them that there was no other name under heaven given among men whereby they could be saved (Acts 4:12). When we returned to the inn a little past 9:00 p.m., all gathered into one small room for a praise service. While we were singing, the innkeeper came upstairs, entered the room, and sat down quietly and bowed his head. He said, "Please sing that song again." We did so, and then he asked who we were, where we were going, and what had brought us to his city.

We talked to him for two hours, for he had never heard of the Gospel. Then all retired, because we had to start on our journey at 3:00 the following morning. This kind innkeeper was up long before we were and had the maids prepare a hot breakfast for us. When we came down the stairs, he met us with a radiant countenance and said, "I prayed to your God last night, and peace came into my heart." We went on our way, rejoicing.

It was some time after noon when we reached Tateoka, where Brother and Sister Shimidzu and quite a number of people met us. What a welcome we received! They had already gathered a number of converts, and when they knew of our coming, this little handful began to tell others. The people walked for miles to the services – up the valley and from far-off mountains.

Tateoka is a lovely little town, and behind it is a mountain. We climbed to the top and counted 42 towns and villages within close range. Down the valley and beyond are more than 100,000 people, unreached, utterly untouched. Here they live and die, without God and without hope.

At our first service, the new converts testified, and our hearts were filled with joy as we heard them tell of the way they heard, then sought and found. We had great liberty in preaching to this crowd. One old woman listened as if her life depended on it. She came to me and said, "I always knew that there ought to be a God like that."

A man stood up at the close of the service and said in such a touching manner, "I have been waiting 40 years to hear what I have heard tonight. I was sure there was nothing in Buddhism that could save me, and I felt that the great God must have some method by which the poor sinner might find salvation."

For three weeks, we visited villages and towns; we walked many miles every day, while the dear people just besieged us for literature. Although we had a large supply, it was soon exhausted and we had to wire for more to be sent from Tokyo. What readers these people are! We must throw in the Gospel seed!

What beautiful spots of nature! Mountains in all their stately grandeur, fertile plains verdant with tea plantations, avenues of feathery bamboo and forests of pine, flowers of the deepest crimson and soft yellow – such were "the footprint and the stamp of God."

But we saw something else as we stood on the crest of the mountain – Satan's footprints. Idol temples dotted the hillsides and the valley, and stone images and wayside shrines lined the roadways. The people who lived in the quaint, picturesque little thatch-roofed homes knew nothing of the Man of Calvary.

Come with me to one of the towns we visited, a quiet town nestling in the foothills of a chain of mountains. The mountains wear their winter robes of snow, and streams of snow water run along the steep gutters to the paddy fields far below. There are not many lands where the people make more use of such tiny streams. Ducks swim in them; little urchins wade and bathe in them; cabbages and carrots are washed in them; buckets of filth are emptied into them; clothes are washed in them; and workers, every hour, dip their pails in them and carry the refreshing contents to the tea shops and homes where tea is brewed. There are no wells here as the people are very superstitious and imagine that if wells were dug, evil spirits would invade the place.

One morning, as we started out over the mountains, we met two old men traveling to the temple at the top. We asked if they had found peace in their hearts. Pathetic was the answer, "I am feeling for the door, but cannot find it."

We had an experience one day that I am sure I shall never be able to erase from my mind. As we walked along from one village to another, we saw a large number of women working in a field. My wife beckoned them to come to the roadside. They dropped their hoes and came, as a foreign woman was a rare sight to them. She asked if they had ever heard of God. Their reply was, "Oh, yes, we have several gods right here in the field, and in that small building yonder are many gods we worship." My wife and her Bible woman told them the sweet story in all its simplicity and charm. They listened intently and soon knelt in prayer by the roadside. It was the first time these dear women had ever heard the name of Jesus.

When we parted, we said, "Remember, the name of the true God is Jesus." They repeated it over and over again, and we left them repeating, "Jesus, Jesus." We walked on a few yards when one of the women came running after us, almost breathless, crying out, "Wait, wait!" When she came near, she said, "What did you say that name was? Tell me his name again." His strange name had been forgotten, but we wrote it on a piece of paper and she hobbled away saying, "Jesus, Jesus, Jesus." I expect to meet that woman in the glory land.

We passed through a large town, and the innkeeper where we stopped for our noon meal kindly permitted us the use of a long veranda for a service. Our little party of workers stood there singing and attracting quite a crowd; for more than an hour we held a red-hot Gospel service. It began to rain, but the people refused to leave. There they stood for another hour under their dripping oilpaper umbrellas. I doubt if even one had heard the name of Jesus before. It was a great privilege.

When we reached the next town, about four miles farther down the valley, the rain had cleared, and we gathered a crowd for an evening service. The innkeepers are most cordial to us, and everywhere we have gone, they have freely given us the use of their large parlors for our services. These are customary meeting places and resemble great banqueting halls. On this particular night, we had about 500 people indoors and more than that out in the large front yard. They were so orderly and quiet that it was a perfect luxury to preach to them. I asked one elderly man if missionaries had visited this town and district. He replied, "About 25 years ago, a man passed through here, but we have not seen one since." These are the things that pull at the heartstrings. It is wearing on the physical to tramp miles every day and hold services almost continually, but –

> It is great to be out where the fight is strong,
> > To be where the heaviest troops belong,
> > And to fight there for man and God.
>
> It seams the face and it dries the brain
> > It strains the arm till one's friend is Pain
> > In the fight for man and God.
>
> But it's great to be out where the fight is strong,
> > To be where the heaviest troops belong,
> > And to fight there for man and God.[13]

There are so many open doors, so many pressing needs, and but one little human life, unable to accomplish one-hundredth part of all we desire! I long to spend and be spent for their salvation.

We made these trips whenever funds would permit, and the result of the sown seed was a harvest far surpassing any expectations. In a short time, after the opening of this first inland station, 17 young men felt a call to the ministry. They were accepted as students in the Bible Training Institute, where they spent several years in diligent study, after which they were sent out as evangelists to their own people.

---

13   Cleland B. McAfee

Chapter 8

Enlarged Borders

Early in 1903, Charles wrote:

> We are seeing a great increase in the most important department of the work – the Bible Training Institute. Our rented quarters are cramped and crowded, and we simply must have our buildings so we can accommodate the large number who are sending in their applications. Some of the finest fellows I have ever met are here in school. They are red-hot after souls. I only wish that you could drop in and attend some of our meetings. The needs are pressing. The work is expanding. The hall was packed last night to overflowing with eager, earnest listeners, and 15 seekers responded immediately when a call was made. I am beginning to realize that the day of small things is now passing … that God has sent us to do business for him in great waters.

> Today, letters were received from 10 young men and 4 young women seeking admittance to our

> Bible Training School. What does this all mean? Here are the applicants and no room to receive them. While waiting before God in prayer this morning, I received this promise: "Enlarge the place of thy tent,... lengthen thy cords, and strengthen thy stakes" (Isaiah 54:2). If we were here under a mission board, we could write to our home council and place our need before them, but we have no home council. To whom shall we go? To the One who has called us to his work. To the One who sent us without purse or scrip. We ask him to look upon this present need and to make room for these students.

God marvelously strengthened and developed the faith of his servant, far beyond the limits of this thinking.

Two months later, on June 8, he wrote to the Telegraphers Band:

> Today is our wedding anniversary. We celebrated it by having a special prayer meeting with our dear Brother Nakada and the students. We prayed for the needs of the fast-growing work and the new building. The meeting lasted from 7:00 in the morning until late in the afternoon, and no one cared to stop for dinner. The students laid hold of the promises, and one of them quoted John 11:40: "Said I not unto thee, that, if thou wouldest believe, thou shouldest see the glory of God?" Fresh assurance that God would give us the needed building came into our hearts. Our treasury was drained this morning, but we held out our hands to our Father in heaven without a shadow of a doubt or a shiver of fear. We

know for certain that he will not fail us, for "God, that cannot lie, promised" (Titus 1:2).

It was a remarkable prayer meeting. Each one present had a strong conviction that God was in the lead of this new advance. Charles suggested that as they had asked according to Mark 11:24, they should praise by faith for the answer. A volume of praise ascended like a cloud of sweet incense, and from that moment doubt never entered his mind.

> Then forward still—'tis Jehovah's will,
> Though the billows dash and spray.
> With a conq'ring tread we will push ahead;
> He'll roll the sea away.[14]

He began at once to plan for the building of a large Bible training institute. Not one dollar was in sight when he began the search for a suitable location. Small tracts of land were available, but every time he attempted to purchase one, some trivial thing occurred that completely blocked the way. The prayerful search continued until one day, Charles, Brother Kilbourne, and several others took a trip to the suburbs of Tokyo, where they found a field of waving grain. The air was soft and balmy. Mount Fuji, with its snow-crowned summit, lay just beyond, and from the slight elevation, they could see miles of country. Here, without doubt, was God's own choice. Funds for its purchase came in answer to believing prayer – no great amounts, but small gifts from many saints scattered far and near.

Charles' ideas for plain but substantial frame buildings were similar to those of the early Quakers who believed in plain meetinghouses and not in lavish expenditures. Not without

---

14 Henry J. Zelley, "He Rolled the Sea Away," 1896.

tests of faith were those buildings erected. The following incident gives a glimpse of one trial and its outcome.

The third payment for the building, $2,000, was due in three days, and there was only $72 in the mission treasury. This was barely sufficient to cover the cost of food needed for our large family of coworkers and students. The day before the payment was due, a steamer arrived from America. The foreign post usually brought a number of letters containing gifts, but this time only one letter came, and in it was a $5 bill.

The workmen were constructing the building, while the missionary and Japanese workers were closeted with God. We were at our wits' end but, thank God, not at faith's end, for faith generally begins at such tight places. Our last hope of help from America seemed to be gone, but as we continued in prayer, the burden on our hearts made a hasty exit as the promises of God rolled in until our mouths were literally filled with laughter. It seemed that God had enabled us to lay hold of his promises. In the course of prayer, one of those present reminded the Lord that on one occasion he had met the need of his own by means of a coin in a fish's mouth. We prayed, "Lord Jesus, You still have fish at Your disposal. You can supply our need in this way even now, for You are still the same."

Another person quoted part of Mark 11:23: "and shall not doubt in his heart,… he shall have whatsoever he saith." Thus, for several hours, one after another mounted up in faith until, at the end, there was a perfect blend, and prayer ended in praise. All watched, waited, and wondered how God was going to get to us the $2,000 before noon the following day. Faith burned brightly in every heart. A definite request had been registered in heaven. Faith claimed the great gift from God, and what was the result? Faith honors God and God honors faith. The clinging hand of his child makes a desperate situation a delight to him.

The next morning dawned bright and clear, and the army

of Japanese workers was on hand early, singing as they worked, for this was payday. Nine o'clock came, then ten, still no answer. Noon arrived, and the simple dinner was served. One quoted Exodus 6:1: "Now thou shalt see what I will do." Each one present quoted some encouraging promise, and faith held fast. At 5:00, about time for the workmen to quit, a messenger boy strolled up the walk, shouting, "*Dempo! Dempo!*" (Cablegram! Cablegram!) The band of missionaries stopped their work to listen to the message, which read, "Two thousand dollars at cable office." The donor was unknown to us.

"And Jesus himself drew near." Tears mingled with shouts of victory. God had not forgotten to be gracious. The little company fell upon their knees and praised him from the depths of their hearts for not permitting them to become a reproach among the unbelievers.

Who timed this to arrive just at the critical moment? Coincidence? The calculation on the basis of probabilities is too difficult. God! How unsearchable are his ways (Romans 11:33). The feeling of his hand upon us gave us great peace, and such experiences are worth all that they cost.

God's hand was so evident during those days. We prayed daily, and the answers were marvelous. We hesitate in telling the public about some answers to prayer for fear that they might be tempted to think these were exaggerated.

The compound under construction consisted of three acres of ground, a large men's dormitory with lecture rooms, a large hall seating 2,000, a women's dormitory, two missionary homes, and three Japanese-style bungalows.

The day of the dedication was memorable. The students, previously packed into the cramped, inadequate quarters in the heart of the city, now lived in new, airy rooms. The faithful teachers, who were pouring their lives out in the Master's service, moved to larger quarters. We opened the splendid hall, which then seated about 500, and began meetings that eventually turned the tide for thousands of lives.

One old Japanese brother, who had prayed with intense interest for the buildings, with tears streaming down his wrinkled face, arose at the dedication and said, "Let us sing 'Praise God from Whom All Blessings Flow.'"[15] The hundreds present at this occasion heartily sang through this doxology three times.

The opening up of this district brought fine business families to the neighborhood. Soon, property soared in price until the location became worth more than 50 times its purchase price. The city borders continue to extend for miles, so it was no longer in the suburbs.

On New Year's Day, 1904, Charles wrote to a friend:

> We are just entering our New Year's Convention, and while reading the Word this morning, John 16:8 made a powerful impression on me. "When he is come, he will reprove the world of sin." That is the secret of revivals. "Not by might, nor by power, but by my spirit, saith the LORD of hosts" (Zechariah 4:6). I feel that absolute dependence upon the presence and power of the Holy Spirit in the conversion of sinners and sanctification of the believers is felt too little everywhere. There is too much dependence on machinery, learning, eloquence, and popular preaching.
>
> May God grant us anointed eyes to see our own nothingness, and may the fire burn up everything human during these days. The voice of agonizing prayer breaks the stillness of the morning. The prayers of some of these precious Japanese are heaven-moving, heaven-opening. What

---

15 Thomas Ken, 1674.

wonderful and striking types of men, what glorious Christians!

At the opening meeting, the spirit of prayer was mightily outpoured, and for several hours, we heard one stream of continuous intercession. Everybody prayed, quite oblivious to one another, when suddenly there came a hush like the receding of an ocean wave and then a time of intense silence when we heard the footfall of the Master, and all returned to their rooms in the hush of his presence. The very atmosphere was fragrant and refreshing.

He wrote of another convention, a few years later:

Japanese workers spent three full days waiting on God before those meetings. Far off in the quiet country, in an abandoned farmhouse, they waited and prayed until all felt that God had heard them and they returned with faces shining. God came in mighty power in the first service. The workers were drawn together in tender love; there were no divisions to be found anywhere. I wish you could have heard them singing "Crown Him Lord of All!"[16] It was like a great wave of praise surging up against the pillars of the throne of God.

Just beyond our compound is a great heathen temple, and the echo must have reached the worshipers there. We had a real foretaste of heaven yesterday. Six hundred were present at the morning service who partook of Communion.

---

16 Edward Perronet, from "All Hail the Power of Jesus' Name," 1779.

After that convention, which 1,000 people attended, Charles was impressed that such a meeting should be duplicated in every city of Asia. He wrote these lines to a dear friend:

> What hath God wrought? My soul is humbled to the dust. Not unto us, but unto God belongs the glory. The converts in the outstations have multiplied beyond all expectations. Multitudes are calling for us to come and bring them the Living Bread.
>
> I meditated this morning on John 6:11 about the lad with five loaves and a few fishes. No miracle was performed until he placed his *little all* into the hands of Jesus. He literally gave his *all*, not one loaf reserved, nor one-half a fish for himself, but after he had done this and the "all" was in the Master's hand, the miracle was performed.
>
> I searched my soul to see if anything remained in my possession that I had not given to God, but found nothing. I have no bread or fish to give, but thank God, all I have has been given to him. We have no reserves anywhere, no bank accounts for a rainy day, no houses or lands. I praise him for this emptiness. I feel that I can ask my heavenly Father for bread for this multitude and he will multiply it a thousandfold. It is not a question of the *supply* in hand, but the Supplier.

These conventions made Tokyo a real Oriental Jerusalem "whither the tribes [of the Lord] go up" (Psalm 122:4). Each year they increased, not only in numbers but also in blessing. In 1927, more than 2,000 attended, and the large hall was enlarged to accommodate the crowds.

Chapter 9

The Promotion of Scriptural Holiness

Scriptural holiness is the blessed truth that helped form early Methodism. Holiness meetings began soon after our arrival in Japan. It became apparent to Charles, as he became acquainted with Christians of every name and creed, that what they needed more than anything else was a measure of spiritual power beyond what they had already realized. Old foundational truths were exclusively relied upon. A desire for further edifying arose in the heart of the national Christians. Life was stirring. The rooting downward was following a shooting upward with a fervent desire for blossoming and fruiting. Tidings of a life of joyous liberty were unfolding, of possibilities of victory and deliverance from sin, and of a life of unbroken service. People longed to hear more. They yearned that their lives might not be a weary existence but an overflow, and they began to "ask the way to Zion with their faces thitherward" (Jeremiah 50:5).

Charles had faith in God and saw a little cloud rising out of the distant sea. He believed that God would raise up Spirit-filled preachers in Asia after the old pattern. He wrote to a missionary, "If the Holy Spirit had been given right-of-way in the church, there would have been no unevangelized part in the earth. The great secret of missions is the Holy Spirit. The great failure of missions is his absence."

After less than a year in Japan, he wrote:

> The holiness meetings have increased in attendance until there is no standing room in the hall. Young and old converts are hungering and thirsting for full salvation. Today, young women from the women's college crowded the altars, and young men from Aoyama College and the Imperial University knelt in groups all over the hall. Some were praying, some were waiting in silence, utterly oblivious to their surroundings, but all in an attitude of expectancy. Some were softly singing, "Let it come, oh Lord, we pray thee … Oh, revive the hearts of all!" We all seemed to be carried right away to a high mountain apart with our Lord.

A month later he wrote:

> "Last night, Nakada San preached for more than an hour and a half, and yet the people lingered as if they did not wish to leave. He stressed the blessing of sanctification, numbers came through to a victory, and there was a shout in the camp. It rejoices my heart to see these new babes walk into the blessing heart-first instead of headfirst. I am so glad that I am here. The only life that counts is that lived for others."

A young student in one of the largest colleges in Tokyo strolled into the services one evening. He was so deeply convicted of his heart's need that before the invitation was given to come forward and seek Christ, he was kneeling at the altar rail, weeping and praying. God met him; he rose from his knees with his face aglow. He returned to college, and in less than a week, he had led 25 of his fellow students to the Lord. An old-time revival swept through that institution.

Two years later, Charles wrote again to homeland friends:

> The Sunday afternoon holiness meetings have increased in attendance, and our hall is filled to its utmost capacity. Japanese pastors and Bible women from the various denominational churches of the city are among the faithful attendants. Last Sunday, the altar was filled, three rows deep, with earnest seekers. I counted 64 people kneeling and seeking to be cleansed and filled. I never heard such praying! One after another arose, with faces aglow, and testified, "He has come!"
>
> One Bible woman of a leading church said, "I have been a Christian for 25 years but my heart has not been entirely satisfied. I have realized a need, and today I made a full and complete surrender of myself to God for time and eternity. All I have, I have placed upon the altar, and according to his Word, I believe that the altar sanctifies the gift." While she was thus testifying, the witness was given to her that the offering had been accepted, and she burst forth into praise that sent a thrill into every heart. This service continued from 2:30 p.m. until 7:00 p.m. and doubtless would have

continued longer, but sinners began to come in, and believers had to return home to make room for them.

Charles believed in a decisive experience of holiness. To an Episcopalian missionary in a spiritual struggle he wrote:

> I sympathize with you in your soul trouble, but if I were in your place, I would not be eternally dying, but would yield myself right up to God and be consecrated forever. It is so easy to keep marching round and round in a beaten path and get nowhere. The reason so many Christians have so much fighting to do is that they do not have one sharp decisive battle to begin with. It is far easier to have one great battle than to keep on skirmishing all your life. I know Christians who have actually spent 40 years fighting what they term their besetting sin, on which they have wasted strength enough to have evangelized the world. Have one big battle, one glorious victory; then shout his praises the rest of your life.

No one could question the purity of Charles' life, the practical embodiment of holiness. "The great beauty of Charles Cowman's life," wrote a well-known Bible expositor, "was its symmetry. He was all over alike. He was a man who never varied, and his steadfastness helped to steady others. I have met with few men so even and constant in their religious walk."

Charles never glossed over anything. When controversy came up, he stated his belief in a clear-cut manner, often proving that "a true witness delivereth souls" (Proverbs 14:25). He was honest in his convictions at every cost. No one ever had a doubt as to where he stood, and he did this with no shadow of bravado or self-assertion but in meekness and wisdom, the sweet reasonableness of Christ. His convictions on the subject of heart holiness were grounded upon a close study of the Word, and he never failed to let his belief in the blessed experience be well understood, often in circles where it cost something to be firm and true.

Charles was never known to compromise the truth for the sake of prestige. He did not forget the purpose of his journey or his life that had been committed to the sacred trust. He never sold the truth to save the hour.

Yet his faith and experience never seemed to separate him from others who did not feel and think as he did. His was a purity that attracted, not one that repelled. He believed it to be possible to be both sane and holy.

A Presbyterian minister wrote:

> "We differed very widely in doctrine, and I have never been able to see sanctification in the way he taught it, yet he saw it in the Book and adorned the doctrine (Titus 2:10). Every honest-minded man is bound to be extreme, and by *extreme*, I mean *definite*. His life influenced me in a peculiar way, which I cannot quite express in words. I wanted to live closer to God after being with him for an hour, and I longed for the deeper life which he ever lived."

Chapter 10

The Advance Into Korea

A map of the Orient in Charles' study had tracings of deep-red letters that denoted populations of countries for which he prayed for years: Korea, China, Thailand, Vietnam, Tibet, Russia, and Taiwan. To his missionary heart, these figures spelled lost souls.

When he returned from deputation tour in America in 1904, three Koreans who had entered the Tokyo Bible Training Institute in his absence – Li, Kim, and Chung – greeted him. They had heard of the school in Japan where students were equipped for aggressive soul winning. Although unfamiliar with the Japanese language, they had been accepted. How diligently they set to work to learn the language, and in a brief time, they spoke brokenly but understood the lectures. After three years, they finished their Bible training, and believing that God meant for them to have a similar school in their own country, they returned, praying that it might become a fact.

The military sometimes sails under sealed orders, not to be opened until the expedition is on its way. When God asked Charles to go to Korea, he said, "It is a part of the original contract to do the will of God as far as he shall make it known, and I accept this new requirement."

The advance was not undertaken without much prayer. Such a burden was not lightly assumed by a man whose hands were already full. Not a dollar lay in the treasury for the opening of such a new and extended work, but God fully assured Charles that he was able to care for the work in both countries and his resources were equal to the new demand; in this faith, it was undertaken.

The word definitely given to him for Korea is found in Haggai 1:8: "Build the house; and I will take pleasure in it, and I will be glorified, saith the LORD," and in 2:9: "The glory of this latter house shall be greater than of the former, saith the LORD of hosts: and in this place will I give peace, saith the LORD of hosts."

God worked in a wonderful way on behalf of Korea! We needed a missionary, and he laid his hand upon two choice souls in England, John and Emily Thomas, and sent them to Korea in 1910 to take charge of the new work.

Through *The Oriental Missionary Standard*, we made known that the Society had extended its borders into Korea and expected to build a Bible training institute there. The news was welcomed, and we received gifts from hundreds of friends. The gifts were not large, but God multiplied them, and there was sufficient with which to purchase the location and construct several buildings.

This step marked another crisis in Charles' life. He was conscious of God's call, and there were countless indications that God was going before us. But, as Charles wrote to a dear friend during those days, "The devil is not put to flight by a courteous request. He meets us at every turn, contends for every inch, and our progress has to be registered in heart's blood and tears." Undaunted by difficulties, he refused to be turned aside from the path of duty.

There was no small amount of persecution. Charles was, at times, acutely sensitive to the sharp criticisms dealt to him through misunderstanding of his motives. He was misjudged and stood under suspicion of false teaching, but he had no new religion, only the age-old Gospel. Accusations made wounds and left scars, but even the scars were soon worn off by the remembrance of his divine Master's tenderness and forgiveness.

There can be no Easter without a Good Friday, and Charles experienced a constant Calvary during the time the foundation was being laid for the Korea Bible Training Institute. The adversary, seeing what was to happen in the lives of these people, did everything to hinder and frustrate the plan. Yet the work advanced in a wonderful manner, and God poured out his Spirit upon the new converts.

"Unless we maintain our standards, the whole work goes down," Charles wrote to a prayer partner.

People in the homelands have little comprehension of the difficulties with securing locations for Christian work in other countries. Intricacies enter into the negotiations, and days, weeks, and months often pass by, even after the location has been found, before the property is transferred.

God gave two promises to Charles as he searched for locations: "They got not the land in possession by their own sword" (Psalm 44:3), and "I will give you the good of the land of Egypt, and ye shall eat the fat of the land. Also regard not your stuff; for the good of all the land of Egypt is yours" (Genesis 45:18, 20).

He had searched two weeks for a suitable location for the Bible training institute, but every available hilltop in Seoul was occupied except one. He bargained for its purchase, but overnight a peculiar circumstance occurred. Someone, upon learning that The Oriental Missionary Society had contracted for that particular site, offered the owner a much larger sum. So the promise was broken. This was a strange test of faith indeed, but God's servant was able to say, "God meant it unto good." Turning the seeming disappointment into his appointment, he began another search.

It came during the intense heat of summer. One morning quite early, while walking through the narrow streets, a Korean gentleman approached Charles with the question, "Are you the person looking for a plot of land for a school?" He replied in the affirmative. The Korean then said, "I am employed in the former emperor's household, and my master has a plot of ground he will sell to you."

Learning where it was located, Charles walked quickly outside the West Gate and climbed the beautiful hill overlooking Seoul. He had a magnificent view of the city there as well as miles of valley, which lay at the right. There was not a lovelier spot in the entire city, nor one better suited for the Bible training institute. It seemed to have stood there for ages, waiting for this time. The air was fresh and pure, far removed from the odors and filth of the valley below. And the price? It was almost less than half of the amount of the smaller location. Incidents like this colored Charles' life with joy.

The next outgoing steamer carried a letter to praying friends:

> Praise God! Today the magistrates came as if by appointment and determined the land boundaries; all the matters were amicably settled. We have the deed to the property in hand, and I have already contracted for brick, stone, and mortar and have engaged masons and carpenters. We begin construction of the building this coming week. By the architect's drawings, which I am sending to you, you will notice we propose to construct substantial

buildings. Such structures could not be built in America for five times the cost of these. We have the most wonderful location, and to think that it has been truly God-given! Every time I step on it, I feel like praising him.

Soon the buildings were up and occupied with splendid young people who had heard the Lord's voice calling them to preach his Word. Charles' cup of joy was overflowing indeed. He lived to see hundreds of young men and women equipped for their life work there. In addition, unlooked-for service opened for his beloved Master. New friends were given, new lessons taught, and many sweet surprises were planned for him by the Lord. The temptation at first to say, "We are not able," must have been very great. But he did not flinch, and all these things sprang from Charles' willingness to "go up and possess the land" (Deuteronomy 9:23).

Work opened up in the country districts patterned after the work in Japan, building churches and opening interior stations. The story of the transformation of whole regions through the power of the Gospel constitutes a thrilling record. By 1927, 57 churches had sprung up and scores of itineration points, while Korea Village Campaign Bands had visited about half of Korea. Seekers in 1927 numbered 5,564.

Charles witnessed the growth of these institutions beyond his most sanguine hopes. But success did not satisfy him nor prompt him to settle down in some quiet resting place. The ascendancy he acquired, instead of making him vain, filled him with awe and increased the rigor of his self-discipline. A few lines found in his papers reveal the man:

> "God must have looked all around to find a stick poor enough to use, and when he saw me, he said,

'Here's one,' and that is why he picked me up. I have never been able to fathom *why* he passed by the many who were seemingly far better qualified but gave me such an important place in the work of training an army to 'build the old waste places:... [and] raise up the foundations of many generations' (Isaiah 58:12); but I humbly and obediently accept the trust."

In retrospect, Charles' career would appear like one unbroken series of successes, but as I retrace his steps in memory, I can testify to the exhausting labors, constant self-denial, and restless activity that ever kept him calling upon the name of the Lord. He rendered his service so joyfully that he was rarely conscious of the mental and physical strain incurred. But many of his friends thought he was undertaking too much and frankly told him so.

They sometimes judged him harshly. "Did he not, by example, encourage the worn missionary to take on what was too strenuous for him?" "Shouldn't powers like his be treated with respect and guarded?" Such were the criticisms. But his life was a torrent of divine intensity as if to illustrate the proverb, "The more light a torch gives, the less time it burns."

Chapter 11

Deputation Tours

A mere glance at the surface cannot estimate the real value of the deputation tours that Charles made. An observer might say that the principal object of such travels was that of raising funds. However, Christians at home who gave of their substance received something that far outweighed their gifts. The joy of the Lord fills the hearts of those who hold their wealth ready to use for God. Charles never tried to obtain unwilling offerings from his audience. He never begged. But he always held before his hearers the lofty privilege of giving to the Master who bids us to lay up treasures beyond the reach of thief, moth, and rust. He enlarged their horizon in respect to the world and gave them a relish for its conquest.

At that time, leaders of the Holiness Movement centered their attention on work in the homelands. They were in danger of losing sight of the Great Commission. Charles' heart was saddened over the fact that God's children often needed a "second conversion" to cause them to take an interest in foreign missions. In many churches where the missionary fire was burning low, God used Charles' simple yet gripping messages to rekindle the embers.

A constant prayer on his lips was, "Oh, that God would burn into Christian hearts the sense of their responsibility to the heathen!" He realized that there was a great lack of knowledge concerning conditions and needs in these lands. Therefore, God's children did not realize their responsibility and could not pray intelligently for the great work. Little did he dream that God would call him to girdle the globe time and time again, spending months in heavy missionary campaigns in America and Great Britain, but this became an ever-widening ministry. The campaigns were strenuous, and he took little rest even during intense summer heat. He had a master passion, and one could not enter his soul-stirring meetings and leave with no belief in foreign missions.

A friend noted, "Whenever the evangelization of the Orient was mentioned, his soul took fire, and you felt he would die through his own zealousness before he reached the sunset of life, and it was so. He belonged to the class of early martyrs, whose passionate souls made an early holocaust of the physical man."

Charles had great faith in the use of missionary maps and seldom held a service without a large map of Asia hanging in some conspicuous place. Once, he had hundreds of small maps printed with mission stations marked in red and sent them to the homeland helpers for their use while in prayer. "No information, no inspiration," he would say.

A missionary worker in the British Isles wrote of him:

> I cannot forget Mr. Cowman and his missionary map. With a pointer in his hand, he would take us from province to province and from city to city, naming the stations which The Oriental Missionary Society had been privileged to plant. Then he would point out the vast districts where hundreds of villages remained unevangelized,

and often he would turn around to say, "Beloved friends, these villages must be reached; they can be reached, and by the grace of God, we mean to reach them."

Leaving the map of Japan, he would take us to Korea and tell of the work in the Hermit Kingdom, first to one station, then to another, until we had visited 50. Again he would say, "What about that great number of people in the villages who will not be reached unless we go to them?"

Then when he had finished with the maps of Japan and Korea, we breathed a sigh of relief, for we felt he was attempting too much for his limited strength. But he continued, "Now we shall leave these two smaller fields and jump over to China, where by the grace of God, we mean to put on a great evangelistic campaign and establish Bible training schools, because our call also includes that far stretch of land."

We were almost ready to say, "Brother Cowman, we have gone just as far as our faith will permit us. Let us go home, think and pray, and we shall come back to the next service."

Calmly and confidently he spoke of the evangelization of China's millions. His faith and expectation made one feel that God was real to him. He was a volcano of conviction, enthusiasm, and activity. His messages were the outpouring of his heart on the subject nearest to it: *The Evangelization of the World in Our Generation*.[17] This was the watchword the church has been so

---

17   John Raleigh Mott, The Evangelization of the World in This Generation, 1901.

slow to adopt. Many earnest missionaries returned to their fields out on the distant battle lines with a fresh vision that the Great Commission "to every creature" *could* be carried out.

Each time a tour was undertaken, there would occur some strange or sudden blockade. These became so numerous that Charles wondered in what form the Enemy would come out against him the next time. During his first furlough in America, he was in a great train wreck, but he was miraculously saved. On his first trip to England, the Suez Canal was blocked, because the ship ahead had been bombed with dynamite. Soon after the *Titanic* disaster, a huge iceberg came floating down and nearly struck his ship.

Once while en route to Japan, he stopped over in Honolulu for a day while the steamer lay in port. He was sitting under a large coconut tree in a park when suddenly he felt impressed to leave. No sooner had he done that when a great limb crashed down right over the chair where he had been sitting.

Once, on the Indian Ocean en route to Britain, a huge meteor fell within a few yards of his steamer. All the hounds of hell seemed to be after him, but God watched over him. How often we quoted the saying, "Man is immortal until his work is done." Some beautiful incidents followed these strange attacks of the Enemy, and usually he would meet someone who would take a special interest in the cause dearest to his heart, the cause of missions.

One summer during a deputation tour in America, a peculiar temptation was thrown in his way. The needs were great, and the Society not well known. The heat was extreme, and Charles was weary and worn. Two letters written to me during those days give a glimpse of God's child under hot fire.

New York City, August 11

My dearest Lettie,

The train was almost forty minutes late, but I arrived in New York yesterday at noon, dusty and weary. The weather is unbearably hot, over 100 degrees in the shade. How the New Yorkers exist through it is a mystery. Surely God never meant that such masses should be huddled up in great cities like this when He has made such vast prairies and plains. Such weary-looking men, tired-faced women, and poor kiddies! How I wish that they might have a whiff of real country air!

After luncheon, I went to the Bible Society's headquarters and met Dr. Haven, who was pleased to see the copy of the marked New Testament in Japanese. He thought the idea was quite unique. When I left the building, I had a distinct impression that it should be printed in Korean also. It will take several thousand dollars to do it, and of course, the Enemy was on hand to whisper, "Where is the money to come from?" Well, we need have no fear whatever about the funds for printing if God has really spoken, so let us keep this before him in believing prayer.

I have something amusing to tell you, as a peculiar temptation was thrown in my way, yet it was not a temptation because I was not tempted with it. I just called it a device of the Enemy.

After I had visited the Bible Society, I went up to the telegraph office to see old friends. I found them in a magnificent new building. You should see their elegant offices. Number one, right down to the last minute, liveried messengers, spick and span for first-class business! Mr. - - - was in an inner office somewhere, as he now holds an important position. When I asked to see him, the clerk looked at me as much as to say, "Who are you anyway?" He doubtless mistook me for an agent and promptly said, "You cannot see him; nobody can."

I handed him my card and said, "Will you kindly hand him this?"

He went away, returning in about five minutes, his face all smiles as he said, "This way, sir." He escorted me through long corridors into an elegantly appointed office, and soon I was in Mr. - - - 's presence.

What a greeting he gave me! I surely thought he would shake my hand off, he was so cordial. His first words were, "Well, Cowman, I have been thinking of you today and wishing I could see you, but I thought you were over in Japan somewhere."

He then told me of their great difficulty in finding capable men for official positions. He was in a great quandary, as some of his principal men had left that very morning. For an hour, he sat there trying his utmost to convince me that I was more needed in the telegraph office than in the mission field. He begged me to stop and help them and offered me a position that fairly took my breath away for the moment. An alluring prospect it was indeed.

Lovely office, luxury, little to do but look wise and draw a large salary every month.

Poor Mr. - - - is still unsaved, and I do covet him for the Lord. You will remember that I used to talk to him a great deal. He is far from the fold. We must never stop praying for him, for God's arm is not shortened.

Are you wondering what I told him? "When I get the Gospel to our 500 million of the Orient, then you may talk to me about coming back to the telegraph service."

The Enemy suggested that if I accepted this position, I might supply the need of the work in that way. But how could I leave those dear people without violating the most solemn convictions of my conscience? I would not exchange my humble toil among them for all the positions of earth, and God knows how to supply the need. Don't overdo this hot weather. Please write every day.

With all my love, forever yours,
Charlie

New York City, August 15

My Dearest,

I was all packed up to leave when your letter came. I went out to a little park near the hotel and read and reread it; I lived a long hour there in that letter with thoughts of you. Perhaps there was some moisture in my eye. I knew that you would say, "Get thee behind me, Satan," when you heard Mr. - - - 's proposition. All the morning, I have been pondering over these words: "He that putteth his hand to the plow and looking back is unfit for the kingdom of God" (Luke 9:62). I know a lot of young men who are out of the ministry because they "looked back."

You and I may not have some things that the world offers, but "Bread shall be given him; his waters shall be sure" (Isaiah 33:16). *Sure* and *shall* are firmer than the rock of Gibraltar, and if God sees fit to bring us into severe tests, he is able to sustain us on such fare, and we shall rejoice and be glad. We are God-called missionaries, and there is no discharge in this war. I would not exchange places with the wealthiest men, for I have learned that I can be rich without money.

How I wish you were here with me. I am like a ship with torn sails without you and have longed that we might pray unitedly over some of these problems. "Oh God, our help in ages past"[18] has been singing itself in my heart, and he will not fail us in this crisis hour. Somehow, I feel that he is allowing the situation to become desperate before he steps in, but we shall wait and pray and he will "shew himself strong in the behalf of them whose heart is perfect toward him" (2 Chronicles 16:9).

I thought of running down to Philadelphia yesterday and spending a day with Brother and Sister

---

18   Isaac Watts, 1719.

Hoffman, but felt that if I did, I might be tempted to tell them about some of our tests, so I remained in and told Jesus.

I went to the Water Street Mission this evening and was scarcely inside the door when the leader invited me to come to the platform and give the message. What a motley crowd, far worse than our old crowds in "Little Hell," but the same type of men. I spoke to them of the love of God, for the poor fellows looked as if they needed a little bit of love. I told them how he had found me, and as I was leaving, a man grasped my hand and, with tears, said, "I accepted Jesus Christ as my Savior while you were talking." It did my heart good. Praise God for one more soul!

The young folks from a Bible institute sang a special song I had never heard before:

> I've enlisted for life in the army of the Lord,
> > Though the fight may be long, and the struggle fierce and hard;
> With the armor of God and the Spirit's trusty sword,
> > At the front of the battle you will find me.[19]

As I walked along to the hotel, I thought of the words in 2 Chronicles 20:15: "The battle is not yours, but God's." And over this promise, my soul rolled its notes of triumph. I slept very little last night. Somehow, the cry of the unbelievers rang in my ears all through the night. Before I retired, I read, "He came and found them asleep" (Matthew 26:43), and the picture of the sleeping church and

---

19 Lelia N. Morris, "At the Battle's Front," ca. 1906.

eternity-bound souls drove the last bit of sleep away.

Let us covenant together anew to do our utmost to bring the lost to Christ, even though it may bring us to early graves. Our lives may be short, but they must be fruitful. I trust this burden may soon be lifted, and we shall be able to go back home, for America has no charms for me.

With all my love, forever yours,
Charlie

How seldom we see souls of this mold. Charles came through this test a positive gainer, for soon there came a complete reverse, when every need was met, when every student's and worker's support had been assumed by friends in the homeland. God had also abundantly answered prayer for the printing of the marked New Testament in Korean.

The rank-and-file donors of the work of the Society were not rich in this world's goods, but they were rich in faith and love. The greater part of their missionary offerings was often the result of rigid economy and the discipline of self-denial. Often indeed, they were the fruit of deprivation and suffering, but they gave the gifts voluntarily in the noble spirit of sacrifice. One was the hard-earned savings of a washerwoman; another was a small sum given by a child, his own money, gladly offered; and also, a bereaved mother sent her child's bank containing a few pennies, once the possession of her now deceased child. These people would preach by proxy in foreign fields.

In the 16th year of the work, the entire amount of money received in response to simple faith in God passed $500,000. In the 27th year, it went far beyond $2,000,000. Eternity alone will reveal the many prayers of faith and the many gifts of faith represented by this sum, which was spent only in direct evangelism.

Such precious funds were a sacred trust to Charles. He was not the kind of man who indulged in extravagance because someone else was paying for it. Self-denial was his habitual rule. Sometimes he would forego perfectly allowable things for the good of others. It was largely due to his close attention to detail that the Society was carried through times of great financial testing without closing a station or dismissing a worker. This mastery of details, coupled with imagination and a broad grasp, made his 25 years of leadership a marvel of management. A noted visitor said, "I count it a privilege of a lifetime to have seen Charles Cowman in his capacity as an administrator of the Lord's money."

With success came recognition. One evening, he was called upon to give an address in a well-known American church in a large city. He was fresh from the battlefront, and the crowds were eagerly waiting for a glimpse of him. As he stepped to the platform, the audience rose, took out their handkerchiefs, and began waving. How did he receive this ovation? A pained look came into his face, and he quietly fell to his knees behind the pulpit and buried his face in his hands. The hardest of tests he successfully met in his humble manner. In his hour of triumph, he remained simply himself. "I have done nothing," was his reply; and the people loved him.

When he left the mission field to go on these tours, he took work with him that would have overwhelmed an ordinary man. Piles of his letters were forwarded, and for strictest economy of funds, no secretary traveled with him. No one understands more fully than I the cost in rest and sleep so that hundreds of letters might have prompt replies. One year he received thousands of letters. Often, after a heavy missionary service, when the clock stuck the midnight hour, he would continue writing.

How many missionaries at their lone outposts were cheered or national workers lifted over some rough bit of road! He wrote to many people at the crisis of their lives. These were not brief letters either, for he kept in close touch with every detail of the work in the field.

God gives a return value for all that is truly sacrificed for his name's sake, and when a man dares to leave friends, home, and country for the isolation of the mission field, he becomes a larger, better personality, with richer feelings, deeper thought, and truer devotion. Losing his life, he finds it. Charles' life seemed to have come to him in Japan. He was happy in the consciousness that he was in the very service and field where God would have him live and labor. Instead of burying himself in this land, he came to a resurrection of himself. Someone remarked after listening to an unusual missionary address, "Is there anything the Orient has not done for Charles Cowman? He has found himself there!"

He was greatly beloved in the homes where he was entertained, and he made everyone feel at ease with his unaffected courtesy and pleasant conversation. And how he appreciated the "Bethany houses," where kind friends took us into their homes, nursed us back to health and strength, and fortified us for future service.

Two American homes very dear to him were those of Mr. and Mrs. Jacob Hoffman in Philadelphia, and Mr. and Mrs. John Kimber in Newport, Rhode Island. Every trip there was a spiritual retreat. To them and their kindness he owed much, and when he left America, he was refreshed, strengthened, enriched with beautiful memories, and in possession of a friendship that was true to the last.

Charles always looked upon himself as only a humble instrument carrying out the will of God. He often said that he was just a connecting link between the churches at home and the work abroad. The Oriental Missionary Society was put on a sound basis in the sympathies of the people, and his strenuous tours made a permanent place for it throughout the entire country.

During these tours, his vision was broadened to include the whole world. Many mission fields and missionaries were on his prayer list. He kept the cause of Christ and the great dying world far above the cause of his own particular organization. His joy was just as great when he heard of missionaries sailing for India, Africa, or the islands of the sea as when they went to his own beloved Orient.

He reveled in missionary biography and sought to acquaint himself with the work of every field. At missionary conventions, he became acquainted with many of the Lord's ambassadors from the four corners of the world, and his missionary enthusiasm increased.

Once, during a summer tour, he was invited to address a large camp meeting on a Sunday morning. He had traveled a long distance to keep his appointment, but on Friday, a dear missionary and his wife from South Africa dropped in. They greeted him with, "And you are here, Brother Cowman?" There was deep emotion in their very tone. They had toiled long and hard in that far-off land but had not witnessed revivals and the visible results.

Sunday morning came with a great crowd assembled to hear an address on the Orient, and Charles went to the platform. He said, "This is a missionary meeting, and I am going to ask my wife to sing 'Dark Africa.'" I wondered why I was not asked to sing "Beautiful Japan," but I did as he asked. When I finished, he said, "We have with us this morning our dear Brother and Sister Fuge from the Dark Continent. I wish them to come to the platform and take the service." They came with tears to plead for Africa while Charles prayed for them without saying one word about his own fields. A few years later, when a friend asked him to what mission field he should send a gift, he replied, "To the Fuges in Africa."

He had a passion for the whole world, and this one instance gives a glimpse of his largeheartedness and his absolute unselfishness, a character trait formed in him by the indwelling Holy Spirit.

Chapter 12

The Call to China

Very early in his missionary career, Charles prayed for China, "a worthy object for a man of great faith," as Ernest A. Kilbourne observed.

In 1907, he and Brother Kilbourne made a trip to China to study the working methods of other societies. They traveled extensively inland, and on their return home, they spent a week in Shanghai. One day, when quite alone in a hotel, a distinct impression came to both of them that sometime in the future the Lord would extend their borders into China. They did not tell each other at the time, but the call was definite, as God gave both men the same Scripture at the same time. During the following 18 years, they frequently commented about this strange experience. They received no further light, but God kept the call before them and bid them to wait for the appointed time. While waiting for marching orders, they prayed.

One evening years later, Charles and I were standing on the balcony of a little inn in the heart of the Hakone Mountain in Japan, watching the play of light and shade upon the great, gray peaks. We had come up to spend a day or two away from the crowded city. These spiritual breathing spaces for uninterrupted communication with God seem necessary now and then to those upon whom he has laid heavy responsibility.

The evening was perfect with twilight and evening bell, soft moonlight, the music of the waterfall, and the fascinating mountain heights. The sun had just dropped behind beautiful Mount Fuji. Stretched out before us was a panorama of exquisite loveliness. The hills seemed to be bathed in heavenly glory, and the hush of heaven rested upon forest and glen. Silhouetted against the sky was a mammoth cathedral, its spire reaching up until it seemed to meet the stars. It was easy to be transported in thought far from this strange house of worship, far from the haunts of men, to hear the sweet strains of the wonderful organ played by invisible hands and listen to an angelic choir chanting an evensong.

Charles paced to and fro on the veranda, lost in this matchless vision, for he loved God's handiwork. Presently, he came to my side, and I felt his strong arm steal around my shoulders. We had been sweethearts since childhood, and this evening, we talked of God's tender dealings with us since we first met and of his marvelous leading since our wedding day. We recalled the hour when the hand of the Lord plainly pointed to the mission fields of the world. How full were our hearts with praises to him for counting us worthy to bear his name before the lost!

Then we fell to musing. Long had we hoped and prayed that it might be the will of God to let us finish our work on earth together and go to our heavenly home *together*.

We talked of the ministry he had given us in beautiful Japan and Korea, and then our conversation drifted to the evangelization of China's millions. China was included in our call, but our work for that land had consisted only of prayer at that point; we were waiting for the moment when he would bid us to launch forth into that great field.

That night a strange question arose in our minds, doubtless

prompted by a letter we had just received from a dear missionary in China; it told of the sudden Home-call of her husband. At the bottom of her message was this tear-blurred sentence: "We had always hoped we might finish our work here *together*, but now I am all alone ... alone in China!" We breathed a prayer for this precious woman so bereft, so brokenhearted; we sensed something of the depths of her loss and utter loneliness in the heart of a great lost land.

Her letter had raised a question that was persistent and troublesome. "Shall *we* be permitted to walk through China *together*?" Neither of us expressed this thought, although both of us were conscious that it was in the mind of the other.

Our conversation about China, great unreached China – her vastness, her lostness, her ringing challenge to the church – continued, when suddenly, Charles exclaimed, "Oh, look! Look! What a wonderful color is shining on the great white cloud floating over Mount Fuji! What is it?"

We went to the end of the veranda, where we could see more clearly the picture that will never fade from memory. Beautiful Mount Fuji, clothed in thick, white snow, had caught the most brilliant light. It shone like melted gold with shadows of pure soft gray across it here and there that flickered and changed continually. A deep crimson cloud hung over its crest, and one cloud of the softest gray divided the golden peak from the mass of cold blue snow and some shadowy rocks beneath, so that alone in its pure, silent glory stood the upper summit of the mountain. And then the other rocky heights seemed to share gradually its warmth of color until they looked as if they were fire that glowed an intense flame-red.

Charles exclaimed, "It is but an hour after the sunset, and this, why, this is the *afterglow*! It is growing brighter! How beautiful! Oh, how rare! Marvelous afterglow!"

Then we were silent and watched until the gold had faded

to silver, and the silver had changed into snowy white, and all the flame-colored rocks had put on an ashen gray, and that radiant scene had faded into the night.

We went to our room in the inn to remember again this lovely scene. But hours later, in the silent watches of that memorable night, Someone seemed to say to me, "Child, you *shall* walk through China, *but not together.*" A cry of agony was on my lips. "Anything but *that* cross, O Lord! Anything but *that!*"

Somehow, the vision of it never dimmed, although we tried to tell ourselves that it was but a dream, the result of tired nerves, or the impression made by the letter we had received that day. Often, I attempted to tell my Lord that Charles was needed in the Society that he had cofounded, that he could not be spared, and that it was impossible for him to go on alone in a land of lost souls.

When the impossibility became a reality, his grace did not fail.

Chapter 13

The Great Village Campaign

One day at sunset, Charles and I climbed a high mountain near a large city in Japan. Weary from the hard climb, we sat quietly and looked out over the broad valley that stretched for miles. In every direction were villages by scores, yes hundreds, *untouched and unreached*. We sat until darkness fell. One seemed to be standing in our midst who said, "Do you see those villages? I have been there today and have seen the brokenhearted people and have stood beside the weary pilgrims as they bowed down before cold blocks of stone, seeking peace. I have longed to comfort the sorrowing and the sin-sick, but I passed by unnoticed – no one was there to tell them of Me." A still small Voice whispered, "Will *you* not go to the villages and tell them of Me, tell them that I care when their hearts ache and break, tell them that I will be their comforter, their Savior?"

Charles said a glad, "Yes, Lord."

During this time, he read again *The Evangelization of the World in This Generation* by Dr. John R. Mott. It was like a winged seed that flew down the years and influenced his life as nothing else could have done. The words *to every creature* took possession of him and burned like a fire in his bones. He prayed over them and asked others what they meant to them. God had said it, and he never meant less than what he said. He would not give his servants an impossible task. Then why had the last commission not been undertaken?

One evening, a little company of our new missionaries met for language study. No one was permitted to speak a word of English during this study hour. A young missionary asked in broken Japanese, "Brother Cowman, have the villagers of Japan been given an opportunity to hear the Gospel? If not, why not?"

The words were like an arrow and pierced his heart. The language-study class quickly became a prayer service. At 10:00 p.m., Charles went to his room, and at midnight was still at his desk. I urged him to retire, but he said, "I cannot. The burden upon my heart is too great." At dawn, he was still at his desk. He greeted me with a cheery good morning and told me that he had met the Lord in the night silence and that he had unfolded to him a plan whereby every person in Japan might be reached with the Gospel in the next five years.

"We have only skirted the borders of Japan," Charles later said to his fellow missionaries. "Eighty percent of the people have never heard one word of the Gospel, and this condition exists after 60 years of missionary effort. There is no need for us to wait for councils, conferences, and committees. To get at the work and do it, that's the thing."

From an overflowing heart, he made this announcement to the little company of missionaries assembled: "We are going to place the Word of God in every home in Japan, and this is the plan that he gave me."

In his businesslike manner, he had jotted down statistics and figures, the number of provinces in Japan, their population, and the number of homes:

Population of Japan..58,000,000
Number of homes..10,320,000
Cost of Scripture portions and expense of workers..$100,000

He planned a systematic campaign. The provinces were to be taken one by one with a force of workers who would visit every town, village, and hamlet – and every home. He believed that 2 missionaries and 10 Japanese workers could visit the homes in one entire province in six months' time. If the force could be doubled and tripled, several provinces could be undertaken at once. He was sure that 50 missionaries and 250 Japanese workers could complete the work in one year. However, only one or two missionaries could be spared for this particular work from our number. The plan seemed audacious for those days, but Charles' faith and vision had grasped it. This plan was God-given and God-inspired, and he committed himself to it in humble and definite faith. He waited until he had light from the Lord, and then he went forward and made no plans to retreat or turn aside. Nothing seemed left but to carry it out.

"I have a strong conviction," he said, "that this is God's set time for the speedy evangelization of Japan. We must act as if we are the only ones to act and wait no longer. In these days of worldwide, colossal business schemes, why not undertake the King's business as something that requires haste and summon every loyal disciple?"

To friends at home he wrote:

> "The Great Village Campaign has been launched, and it is the subject of much comment throughout missionary circles. It was quickly noised abroad that The Oriental Missionary Society, a "faith mission" with no guaranteed funds or influential home committees, a mission that would not go into

debt even if worst came to worst and nothing was in the treasury, had undertaken to place the Gospel into 10.3 million homes in Japan."

After a thing has been done, everyone is ready to declare it easy, but before it has begun, it is called impossible. Someone said, "What can Charles Cowman be thinking?" The news of the vast undertaking created a thrill of surprise and wonder in the homeland.

We received letters of both encouragement and discouragement. To the latter he boldly replied, "Faith will be staggered even by loose stones in the way if we look manward; if we look Godward, faith will not be staggered, even by inaccessible mountains. 'Go forward' is the voice from heaven, and 'God with us' is our watchword."

In retrospect, his coworker, E.A. Kilbourne, wrote of this venture and commented on the prayer life of Charles Cowman:

> Again, we hear Brother Cowman pleading, and now the burden of his soul is the Great Village Campaign. To reach every creature in Japan was the desire of his heart. "Impossible," the Enemy insistently whispered. Just think of the millions of homes in this empire of 60 million people. Think of the congested cities with their interminable alleys and the great mountains everywhere that must be crossed. Think of transporting literature to the innumerable villages of the far interior and the inhospitable reception one will meet among fanatical idolaters. Think of the lack of hotel accommodations in the country districts and a hundred other difficulties that presented themselves to that pleading soul and how they were magnified into mountains!

But Brother Cowman knew God as the author and fulfiller of all his promises. Mountains must be cast into the sea, trees rooted up, every valley exalted, and every hill made low before this man on his knees, and thus it was. How he delighted in the Word! He took special gratification in pleading that series of promises containing those remarkable and illimitable words – *Whosoever, Anything, All things* – and entered into the realm of impossibilities to seek God, and he always found him there.

The zeal that burned in Charles' heart gradually communicated its glow to others. They too took up the slogan, "The Gospel in every home in Japan during the next five years."

Warmhearted friends who knew his physical limitations urged him not to attempt it; they feared it would result in a complete breakdown, but he felt that God had called him. He responded with unquestioning obedience, and if ever any person on earth attempted to pay his debt to the world, it was Charles Cowman.

"What if we lose our lives in the undertaking?" he said to me. "Be it so, thank God! None of these things move me, neither count I my life dear to myself."

The day of advance dawned, and he responded to the call. The Great Village Campaign was no longer a venture but a fact.

It was undertaken with $5 in the treasury and faith in God. The first distribution of Scriptures began in Tokyo, and workers visited the homes of 3 million people. Workers then went out into the provinces. At the end of four months, the first province, composed of more than 1 million souls, had been reached with the printed message, and 900 had flung away their idols and sought Christ. Letters began to pour in from hundreds of people. Thrilling news came from a little band of workers that tramped daily to hundreds of homes where the Word of God was received with gladness. Seekers and converts were everywhere, hundreds of them amid raw heathenism.

Funds began to come from the homeland – small amounts, but gifts watered with prayers and tears. An added corps of workers undertook the distribution of the Scripture in another province. At the close of three months, when another million people had been given one chance to hear the Gospel, the report from the village workers read, "The work closed in a blaze of glory. We have seen 1,200 seeking Christ. Scores have prayed through in their homes. What a hallelujah march we had around that province until the walls fell flat!"

The Enemy contended for every inch of ground, and pressure of every conceivable kind was brought to bear upon this movement. There was no scarcity of workers, for earnest young Japanese felt the call and heartily responded, but funds began to fail, and it looked as if the Great Village Campaign was at an end. What was to be done? Only one thing – pray. We learned new lessons in trust as we leaned upon the strong arm of God alone. And while we were trusting, God was working. A fresh burden for the evangelization of Japan came upon the hearts of hundreds in the homeland, and the small gifts of the many were laid at the Master's feet.

The time came when we needed larger gifts if the work was to advance speedily. A fine old southern judge tossed upon his bed one night, sleep having escaped him. He had received a letter from his friend Charles Cowman, and the villagers of Japan seemed to be standing about him. Would he dare to leave them to perish for the lack of help he might give? And what about his missionary friend out there who had given up everything to go to the lost? The judgment would have no terror for him, for without hesitancy he could lift his face to God and say, "I have done my utmost." The word in Ezekiel came forcibly to the judge: "When I say to the wicked, Thou shalt surely die; and thou givest him not warning,… [he] shall die … but his blood will I require at thine hand" (Ezekiel 3:18).

Judge Strouse knew his Lord's voice. He rose at dawn, went to his desk, and wrote:

> "My dear Brother Cowman,
>
> My heart is stirred over the work you are doing in giving the Gospel to those who have never heard. Will you evangelize one entire province for me? I enclose a check for $3,000 for this purpose."

Over in Japan, the weary missionary received the letter, which brought new hope and courage to press on. Workers entered the great province of Saitama, and Charles wrote to his good friend:

> Our village campaign bands began their work in Saitama Province last week by distributing a large number of Scripture portions and tracts. The first day, we preached twice in temples, the priests giving us a royal welcome. One of the old priests said, "I believe that what you have told me today is the truth and that my efforts to lead my people for the last 25 years have been altogether in vain. I have led thousands on the wrong roadway, and now I wish to learn the real truth that I may begin even now to turn them into the right road."
>
> The second day of work, 12 young men grasped the plan of salvation clearly. Five old men said, "Stay with us in our village and teach us more." Ten of our workers were out all day and returned at night with glowing reports; we feel abundantly encouraged.
>
> The following report will give you a glimpse of a day's work.

May 2: A cloudless morning. Before starting down the valley to the village homes, we had a precious season of prayer with the workers. One broke down and wept as we sang "The Ninety and Nine."[20] He said, "Not only the one sheep in my country is far off from the gates of gold, they are here by the millions." Thank God that we are out searching for them, and he is helping us to find them.

One band of workers entered a town and held a street meeting. The leader of the young men's club became so interested that he invited them to hold a service in the club room the next day. He sent out personal invitations to all the members, and 50 came – bright, young fellows, all Buddhists. Five of these publicly sought the Lord and knelt simply before their fellows, confessed their sins, and called upon God to save them. They told us that if we would send a preacher, they would open the club room for services free of charge. What calls from everywhere! Would that we had a thousand Japanese preachers ready to thrust into this white harvest. They are the only hope for the evangelization of their land!

In one place, the town council was in session, and a large crowd of people gathered. Business was suspended for an hour and a half so the people could hear the story of Jesus. Five sought the Lord right there.

In another town, the village bands found that policemen of the entire district had met for a

---

20   Elizabeth Cecilia Clephane, 1868.

convention. The chief courteously invited the band to hold a meeting with his men. They sat quietly and listened to the Gospel story; then the chief arose and, with much dignity, said, "Will you please stay with us and teach us more? We need such a message, one that will help our people stop sinning."

The worker asked them to fall upon their knees and he would pray to the living God for them. Every one of them obeyed, simple as little children, while the chief prayed, "O God who lives in the heavens, please come and save us from our sins." When he arose, his face was wet with tears.

These weeks stood out above all others in Charles' life. It was a time of mighty visitation of the Spirit, and entire villages were swayed as a field of wheat is swayed before the passing of a mighty wind.

When the distribution in Saitama was completed, he wrote again to Judge Strouse:

> "Through your gift we have been able to carry the blessed Word of Life to approximately 1,436,895 souls. Hundreds have sought God, and we can report many genuine conversions. It has occupied four months' time. Many splendid outstations and centers have been opened. The cost has not exceeded $3,300."

This reply came from the judge: "I have found no better place to invest my Lord's money and have decided to evangelize another province." A check for $2,000 was enclosed. He further stated, "I will stand behind you until the entire land of Japan is reached." But this was his last gift. God had another plan, and before the distribution in the second province was completed, he was suddenly called Home.

The children of America and England wanted to have a part in the village campaign and sent $3,000 for the evangelization of one province. The women also took it upon themselves to have a share, and 1,000 women sent $5 each as a love offering. Five dollars was sufficient to purchase Scripture portions and pay the workers' traveling expenses; thus, one large or two small villages were reached with the Gospel.

A number of friends heard of this widespread campaign and wrote to inquire about the results of the Scripture distribution. Charles responded with comprehensive statistics, including the following:

> Population of Japan latest census, about: 57,976,322
> Of these we have reached: 35,047,971
> Number remaining to be reached: 22,928,531
> Number of houses in Japan, about: 10,376,700
> Number already visited, about: 6,234,792
> Number remaining to be visited: 4,141,908

He went on to share:

> The area we are to cover is 161,000 square miles, including about 4,000 islands, all mountainous. We have covered more than half of the territory. Between 5,000 and 6,000 names of seekers have been sent in to headquarters in Tokyo. Thousands of others have been dealt with.
>
> Hundreds of New Testaments have been sold

or given to those who received a "portion" and wanted more. We have received hundreds of letters from inquirers, and we have sent hundreds of replies, together with thousands of other tracts and periodicals, to seekers to instruct and lead them. We preached thousands of sermons in the open air, hotels, and halls. In fact, Japan is being literally sown with Gospel seed.

And all this has been accomplished for $55,000. All has been done in answer to your prayers and ours – praise God! Balance needed – about $45,000.

This pioneer work proved to be much more difficult than Charles had ever dreamed. The year 1914 was rapidly nearing its close when funds went down to the last penny. Scores of splendid Japanese workers were offering themselves for the village campaign. They too were longing to plunge into the battle, but they faced an empty treasury morning after morning. Hard work, heavy responsibility, and the impossibility of any escape were telling on Charles' health. The new year began in a semi-breakdown, and fearing it would be complete, he left Japan for America for a short time. The ocean voyage so invigorated him that he was able to be out in deputation work in a few days.

After a few months in the homeland, during which he was busy in conventions and camp meetings, traveling thousands of miles and speaking in hundreds of places, he bade farewell to his friends with a buoyant heart and set out for the field of his labor as one leaving a foreign land for a loved and longed-for fatherland. In a peculiar sense, he felt he was going home. A friend who accompanied him to the steamer said, "Brother Cowman, I fear that you will never come back."

His quick reply was, "I do not need to come back."

Charles returned to his task with unabated diligence. He started out this new year with the thought deeply implanted in his heart that if the village bands could be increased to 100 workers (10 new missionaries and 90 Japanese workers), the entire work could be completed in one year. He prayed, "Lord, send 100 laborers," and in a remarkable manner, the Lord answered that prayer. Almost immediately, 10 splendid young men in America came forward and 90 Japanese men.

During 1917, the bands were engaged in the most intense activity out in the villages of Japan. How persistently they pressed their way through rice plains, over mountains, and through swollen streams in the dead heat of summer and the piercing cold of winter. Millions heard and responded to the Gospel message.

The Great Village Campaign had become well known and was talked about everywhere in pulpits, camp meetings, and homes. People wanted to hear more, but Charles had little time to make notes. He worked in haste.

In the spring of 1917, a temporary headquarters was established on the large island of Kyushu where 9 million people lived. To a prayer partner, Charles wrote:

> We have entered the fourth year of the village campaign. This morning, I remembered all the ways the Lord has led us, and I was moved to tears … tears of joy and thankfulness to our wonder-working God. How I thank him that he has given grace for these heavy years. The evangelization of the world is our Lord's dearest purpose, and he will not fail to supply us with resources as we cooperate with him. I never took hold of the work with more faith and unshaken confidence of success than at this time. Jesus *shall* reign.

Refreshing news came this morning. The distribution work in 12 more large counties has been completed. The number of seekers startled me. I read of more than 400 souls seeking Christ in the last 30 days. This alone compensates for all the scoffs and jeers of those who said, "It cannot be done," and "It will not pay."

One missionary was out in the mountains when he came upon one home where he discovered a cage built of poles in a corner of the garden. Peering through the bars was a fine-looking young man, apparently suffering mentally. There were no facilities in these far-off country places, and the distressed parents had confined him there to keep him from doing violence to others. The missionary gave him a Scripture portion, and the young man called after the missionary, "*Arigato, arigato*" (Thank you, thank you). The missionary's heart was so touched that he began to pray earnestly for him.

After a time, the missionary passed by on his return down the mountain near dusk. He heard a voice in prayer. The young man had read the Scripture portion, its truth had taken hold upon him, and he was calling upon God at the very top of his voice. As the missionary descended the mountain, the night grew still, and he reached the foot of the mountain. But the sound of the young man, still at prayer, echoed down through the cliffs.

As work on Kyushu progressed, Charles shared this update:

> Every member of our bands is keenly alive to the urgency of the work. Although many of the provinces are mountainous and difficult, they are marching on victoriously with the view to complete the work by Christmas.

> The work has extended over most of five years, yet the amount accomplished during the past year since we have had the means for the large force of workers has been remarkable. The 10, sometimes 12, missionaries and their Japanese counterparts have gone over almost half of the Empire during the year, walking over 50,000 miles, equal to twice around the world – over mountain paths and muddy rice fields in all kinds of weather. It has not been easy on the physical, but we have proved how simple the task is that was given to the church in the last great commission of Jesus Christ – to go into all the world and preach the Gospel to every creature.

When the work on Kyushu was completed, the village bands traveled by train and boat to the extreme north, the great island of Hokkaido. The work there had a good beginning with high expectations of giving the Gospel as witness to the 2 million souls living there.

Orders for Bibles, seven or eight a day, came from outlying districts. A young man wrote, "I received a Scripture portion, and it was the first time I ever heard that there was a true and living God. I want him."

Another wrote, "I received a Scripture portion and read the wonderful words that led me straight to him, the Way, the Truth, and the Life."

A few weeks later, Charles wrote:

> "From snow-capped Fuji to coral-reefed Loo-Choo, neglected people are coming by the hundreds to the Savior. The pure Gospel message, accompanied by faith and prayer, makes converts anywhere and

everywhere, even where idolatry has held undisputed sway for centuries. Another notable thing: the greatest success has not been attained by the greatest of our preachers. It has not been the fruit of skilled labor. The simple story, told in a simple manner, has brought the hundreds to the feet of Jesus."

One of the greatest tests during the Great Village Campaign occurred during this time. The treasury again became depleted. One hundred men were out campaigning. "No funds" were the words in a wire from Tokyo. "Lord, to whom shall we go?" was often on Charles' lips. Where? To his never-failing Friend. To the One who said, "Go ye ... to every creature" (Mark 16:15). And he had gone. Could God fail him? Perish the thought!

Telegrams were sent to each band, and on Sunday morning, they sought the Lord in earnest prayer. On Monday, each leader received a note of victory. "We prayed through," wrote one.

"God gave the assurance," wrote another.

Charles had spent the night alone with the Lord, but there had been no wrestling. A deep settled peace stole into his heart, and an assurance came that God heard his prayer and the answer was on the way.

That morning brought a wire from Tokyo. "Dr. Blackstone has cabled $8,000 for the village campaign." (W.E. Blackstone was the author of *Jesus Is Coming*, a book that Charles devoured.) What a doxology of praise rose from grateful hearts!

Charles' most trying fight was not with funds but with ill health. Loving friends who knew about his battle wrote, "Come home and take a good, long, well-earned rest."

But Charles was gazing into the homes where precious souls were living and dying in the darkness. How often he said, "Christ can scatter the darkness if his children shall speed forth with kindled torches." He wrote to a relative, "How can I do otherwise than what I am doing?"

Rest? Settle down in the homeland? Impossible for such a man as Charles Cowman, but he was always so cheerful, so happy, that it was difficult for anyone to believe that he was overworking. Yet in my heart, I had misgivings as to how the end would come. When we were away together, a rare experience for us, he would admit me into the wonderland of his inner hopes, his plans for the extension of the work, his ideas about the evangelization of the Asian people. I always looked forward to such times, for he always had new plans and wonderful things in his heart to reveal. The burden of souls was always with him. He never slipped from beneath it for one moment, and it remained with him to the very end of his days.

One Sunday morning when we were far up in the mountains with our workers, he suddenly said to me, "I feel very ill."

I hastily summoned a doctor who said, "You had better stop right now and return to America." Charles' heart was ceasing to function properly.

There seemed to be no one to take his place, and he believed that, with care, he might be able to continue a few weeks longer. A passage of Scripture made a strange impression upon him at this time; the words were like a diamond flash: "The hands of Zerubbabel have laid the foundation of this house; his hands shall also finish it" (Zechariah 4:9). His own name seemed to be written in this text.

He continued to work, but his private diary told of his battle with pain:

> "August 15 – Experienced a strange pain in my heart in the night, but prayed and it left me. I can see no place to stop in the work.
>
> August 20 – Fight on my soul till death. God grant

that 'I hope to see my Pilot face to face, when I have crossed the bar.'"[21]

And the next day he said to me, "It will be so wonderful to look into the face of Christ – to see the same face that we have seen throughout all our earthly pilgrimage, the Christ with whom we have grown so sacredly familiar out here during these 20 years. He will be the very One who will meet us when we cross the boundary line."

With the autumn of 1917, the Great Village Campaign was nearing completion. But the leader was worn out. After much prayer, we decided to leave Japan for a few months.

Those who were present in Tokyo during his last week there never forgot his closing ministries. Though extremely weak, with his usual self-forgetfulness he was planning for the work. His words of counsel, his prayer, his benediction – all seemed prophetic of a veiled but most fitting farewell.

The final parting was in the early morning. A group of workers and students came to our home from their prayer meeting. He bade them farewell with his old cheery smile, assuring them that he would soon be back at his post again. But those who were left had a premonition that they would see his face no more. They had heavy hearts too deep for words as he left his Tokyo home for the last time.

We boarded the steamer, but she lay in anchor all day. Numbers of friends came to bid him farewell. It was night when the ship lifted anchor and put to sea, and his last look at Japan was under the stars in the moonlight. He watched the receding shoreline for a long time, as it grew fainter. A tear dropped upon my hand in his. Then he hurried to his cabin to pray with great sobs for the brethren he had left behind.

On the first page of the January 1918 *Oriental Missionary*

---

21 Alfred, Lord Tennyson, "Crossing the Bar," 1889.

Standard was the word *HALLELUJAH!* in one-inch, outlined letters. In part, the accompanying article read:

> The Japan Village Campaign Is Finished
>
> By the time this reaches our homeland readers, the great work of taking the Gospel to every home in Japan will have been completed. We may not have time to stop and celebrate, for the very momentum of its joy, its privileges, and its newly revealed responsibilities and results has pushed us right over into the beginning of a similar campaign in ripe Korea, where about 10,000 homes have been reached already. All you who have made this work possible, shout the victory with us and give Jesus all the praise that the nearly 60 million people of Japan have had the Gospel put into their homes. Added to the marvelous ripeness of this Empire is an infusion of the Word of God that awaits the touch of fervent prayer to set this land aflame with a mighty revival. As we shout the victory and earnestly pray for the sown seed, let it be while we advance, and let us altogether mingle with our shouts and prayers the faith-inspired cry, "On to Korea!"
>
> The area of Japan is about 161,000 square miles, and our workers covered it all. The total cost was around $100,000, received in answer to believing prayer. As to the results, the day shall declare them. We leave them where Charles Cowman would have wanted them to be left – at the feet of the Lord.

Chapter 14

Music in the Solitudes

Why not leave the story of his life just as it stands to this point – bright and beautiful, full of life and glow? I would be untrue to my subject if I were to omit the deep shadows which give the picture balance and tone. Once, in the mountains of Japan, we heard a simple melody played on a bamboo flute. Touches of brightness here and there faded into a sadness that was indescribably sweet; we heard a strain of melancholy about these notes, all played in a minor key. As the sweet sound reverberated and filled the air with echoes, we asked each other, "Does God speak in the solitude? Can he make his voice heard in the lonely places?" Yes, God has often talked to his own and revealed himself in the solitudes as he could not have done in the midst of busy crowds. He can use the barren wastes as sounding boards for his own voice. And so, these things are recorded that some child of his in lonely deserts may catch the echo of a wonderful note of triumph and through it may learn to discover streams gushing forth in the desert place.

At home Charles apparently regained his health for a time, but when numerous calls for missionary meetings came, they proved too much for his fiery spirit. He attempted to answer them all. For six months, he traveled incessantly, meeting crowds of people. He looked the picture of health, but the candle was slowly burning down.

He was traveling from a summer camp meeting near Toledo, Ohio, to Owosso, Michigan, when a severe heart pain seized him, and he was unable to proceed. We summoned a doctor who said, "You must stop your public work at once. Return to California and rest."

Charles obeyed the doctor, but the heart attacks continued, and he faced the fact that he was an invalid. I marveled at the way he received the blow, but found his secret long afterward penciled in his diary: "We had the sentence of death in ourselves, that we should not trust in ourselves, but in God which raiseth the dead" (2 Corinthians 1:9).

Charles was great as a businessman; he was great before his audiences; he was great on the mission field. But he was greatest when he was shut away alone with God in the loneliness of the desert. All the interests that had been dear to him were now shut out of his life, but he never lived so deeply, so triumphantly, as during those last six pain-filled years.

I shall always thank God for the privilege of being close by to witness the anointing upon his life in the twilight hour. A small bungalow was now the sphere to which he found himself restricted. Many battles were fought within the narrow confines of that home, but they were not battles against the will of God. At times heroic martyrdoms are not associated with the momentary flash of sword or flame, but with the slow agony of shattered nerves, throbbing brain, and sleepless nights.

"I find it difficult to realize," Charles wrote to a friend, "that I am a real prisoner, but thank God, a prisoner of the Lord. This trial may turn out to the furtherance of the Gospel and I am resting in Romans 8:28."

Only once can I recall his giving way to anything like discouragement and that was when he first broke down. His sister called to see him. He lay quite still. A tear trickled down as he said to her, "It is so very difficult to lie here absolutely helpless when so much work remains to be done." After she left he said to me, "Oh, forgive me for saying what I did. It sounded as if I were murmuring, and God knows I did not mean it that way."

God gave triumph. Charles found it was possible to bless God in the darkest hour, and he stood still in the shadow of the cross. One of the things for which he prayed more than another was that he might be rich in faith, and God sent him to the school where the lesson is taught. He answered his prayer in his own way; he permitted him to be shut in with himself and delivered him with a mighty hand. To a friend he remarked, "I am in the University of Quietness under the Master Teacher."

If the adversary sought to destroy a chosen vessel by that bruise, he was disappointed. Indeed, it was that stroke that gave the weapon the edge and point and that temper and polish, without which it could not have done its proper work.

Every morning was a miracle of resurrection, and the beginning of each new day was like rising out of death. Launching forth each morning required what seemed an impossible effort and needed an unimaginable faith. Charles never had a night of whole, unbroken sleep throughout the six years, and the nights were filled with unutterable agony when the heart attacks would seize him.

There was nothing of the morbid invalid about him. He went out daily for a short walk. Someone in the neighborhood saw him pass by and inquired who he was. A neighbor's boy replied, "Don't you know him? He is the smiling invalid who has heart trouble and faith in God." His most prominent characteristic was radiant cheerfulness. He had set his face toward the sunrise and refused to look on the dark side; even when pain made deep marks on his body, he still claimed the title of "smiling invalid."

After six shut-in years, he said, "These have been the best years of my lifetime, and I believe the most fruitful. Doubtless more has been accomplished for my Lord than when I was in my most active days."

The little brown bungalow became a real missionary center. Missionaries came and went frequently, and meeting them was one of his great joys. But these were times of pain as well, when parting time came and they were waved off at the steamer. None but the Master knew how Charles' heart yearned to be off with them.

Although broken in body, he kept an oversight of the home office and every department of the work on the field, dictating letters by the hundreds. They were so full of old-time fire, cheer, and enthusiasm that they hardly seemed to come from a hopelessly sick man. With his exceedingly limited strength, he made an appeal to the strong to keep the missionary vision – not to grow cold or lukewarm in the task of evangelizing Asia.

Nothing cheered him more than letters from workers on the field, although they added fresh fuel to the fire that was already consuming him. Letters from Nakada always added fresh fire, and the old longing to be back with him returned again. Usually it was some time after reading these letters before he would be able to settle down to rest and relax.

I found it difficult to watch Charles during those days as he clung to the work in spite of his pain and our protests. But Asia, with its deep needs, was on his heart, and he could not forget it. Once I found him in his study with his face buried in his hands, weeping bitterly. On his desk was a map of Asia that was stained with tears. There was a fresh battle and a fresh victory. Again, he was able to say, "Not my will but Thine be done." This was greater than calming the seas or raising the dead. To do God's will is still the highest form of faith, the most sublime Christian achievement. It is spiritual success at its crowning point.

There are few more severe tests of character than pain, but while we cannot change the suffering, we can be conquerors. Between the pages of one of his books, I found a card bearing a few lines in his handwriting. The card was worn, and the words revealed what must have been uppermost in his mind: "He endured, as seeing him who is invisible. Endure when there is every external reason not to endure."

In the stillness of his forced retirement, Charles began to form plans for an advance into China. The call to China had been upon his heart for years, and now something whispered to him that God's time was near. A map of China hung on his study wall, but it also hung in his heart; he prayed in faith for province after province, walled cities, destitute districts, villages, and hamlets. He spent hours and hours praying for China's millions, as a foundation was being laid for the new work. But the time did not seem favorable since China was then war torn.

Yet in 1924 he wrote, "I have the fullest faith in God that he will enable us during the coming year to launch forth and plant the banner of holiness on China's soil." In his vision, he walked over the unbuilt walls of a Bible training institute in that land. His eyes had seen room after room before one stone was set upon another, for he had prayed clear through about the building of this training institute. Those prayers are doubtless the greatest work of Charles' life, the "finish" of the work to which God had called him. How much the work of intercession is discounted, when it is by far the most important of all the dealings with God for men!

Charles showed a visitor the map and led him for an hour through the great untouched places of spiritual need, far from the beaten trail, where millions of souls would be forever lost until someone would go quickly and tell. Across the map he had written in bold strokes, "Without God and without hope: 450 million eternity-bound souls for whom I am responsible." To his visitor he said, "What must the Master think as he looks down upon this map? What must he think of me?" This was his spirit, always taking the blame for this terrible condition.

Letters came from workers in Japan and Korea that told of young Chinese students who had heard of our Bible training institutes and had sought admittance in order to carry the Word of God back to their own countrymen. Charles noted in his diary, "I feel so unequal to the task allotted me, but the work is God's, and I can only look to him that he may glorify his name in his own way. China's age-long night must end. Christ has begun to besiege this ancient and strong fortress, and the work to which he has set his hands will assuredly prosper. We shall reap if we faint not. The Bible training institute will be built, though I may never see it."

Six months before his Home-call he sent out a special letter to friends, told them of the plan, which had widened to an undreamed-of scope, and challenged them to come to the help of the Lord against the mighty. "We are not working against uncertainties, nor afraid of the results. We have tested the power of our weapons," he wrote. With God's promises, he felt secure, even as an invalid. He was also impressed with the thought that though David had the desire to build the temple, he was allowed only to make preparation for it, but his son Solomon was appointed to build it. He said, "God will raise up others to carry out our plans."

Charles' faith in God's power to heal never wavered throughout the six years. He fought day and night with what he considered unbelief that prevented the healing touch, for he believed that something must be lacking in his prayers. He spent days and weeks searching the Word, and he kept on praying; indeed, every breath was a cry for life for his broken body. When the best physicians told him plainly that he could never hope to recover, he only smiled and replied, "But they do not know that God can heal when the case is impossible."

Often Charles attempted to act out his faith, and taking a few feeble steps, he would walk slowly for a block or two. Then the heart weakness would seize him, and he would sit on the curbstone for an hour or more, waiting for strength enough to return home. It was plainly not God's will to heal him, though thousands were praying for him.

One night the Enemy came in like a flood and suggested to Charles that God did not care and that he had been clearly picked out as a target while ungodly men walked about free and well. A great pressure rested on his spirit. Not a word passed between us throughout the long night, but silent prayers went up unceasingly. Near dawn, these words came to his mind: "I have prayed for thee, that thy faith fail not" (Luke 22:32). It was as if the Master himself had slipped into the room and reached his own loving hand down to his sick child.

"Blessed is he, whosoever shall not be offended in me" was a Scripture verse that greatly comforted Charles' heart (Matthew 11:6). John the Baptist was in a miserable prison and heard that Jesus was raising the dead and healing the sick. Most naturally, he must have thought that if Jesus could do that, he could surely get him out of this prison. Why didn't he do it? What grace it must have taken not to question why he who possessed such mighty resources would leave him there, undelivered, in that dungeon! But Jesus left John right there with no explanation.

If we are to enjoy a close walk with God, we must leave many things unexplained. We do not understand everything, but "what I do thou knowest not now, but thou shalt know hereafter" (John 13:7). God could take burdens out of our lives, and yet he does not. That is just the point where hearts break. Christ has all power, and yet he does not mention one word to us of deliverance. These are the hours we will study with delight and amazement in the light of eternity: no explanation; faith nourished; the prison doors left closed; and then the message, "Blessed is he, whosoever shall not be offended in me."

Christ did not deprive John of the unspeakable blessedness to which those come who take no offense. Had he explained, he would have robbed John forever. Let us never press God for an explanation. John did much for Jesus, but the greatest thing he did was to be willing to remain in that prison, *an unoffended soul*. That will probably be his supreme honor.

What about the fulfillment of the Word, "If any man will leave houses and lands for My sake and the Gospel's, he shall receive a hundredfold"? Did this poor faith-missionary come to lack when he lay helpless and broken, no longer able to serve? Ah, no! It was then that the Master came forth and carried him.

When the break came, we had rented a house in Los Angeles where for seven months the battle for life raged. One day, we received a notice that the house had been sold and we would be expected to move in a few days. But where? God only knew the storm that broke so suddenly upon our defenseless heads. Yes, he did know, for the following day, the bungalow at 256 South Hobart was in our possession, and Charles said in his daily prayers, "God bless my beloved friend, Charles E. Sawtelle."

Another friend sent a gift with which to purchase an automobile since Charles could walk so little. Four months later, he received a letter from a Japanese worker, telling of a great need at one of the interior stations. As he prayed and wept, he saw a way of meeting the need. The Ford was sold, which supplied the station with another worker. However, the short trips in fresh air that Charles had enjoyed each passing day were discontinued.

All was not shadow under the discipline of daily dying. Sorrow and joy walked hand in hand. He was in a place to prove the faithfulness of God. True Christian friends are among the Lord's choicest gifts in the pilgrim's path. A rich man is he who stands possessed not of lands or gifts or gold, but of the love of noble souls. Throughout his long illness, kind friends kept his desk covered with comforting, cheery letters. Often was his heart comforted by a letter or visit from his friends, and when the cross grew too heavy to be carried alone, God sent friendly helpers to him.

God tenderly cared for him through those broken years, and nothing touched his heart more than the outpoured love of the Japanese brethren. They occasionally sent him a gift to help cover expenses. Japanese friends in Los Angeles kept him supplied with the choicest flowers, among them the deep-red California rose, his favorite. What a beautiful thing is Christian love.

But his life was drawing to a close, and in his usual, well-ordered manner, he made quiet preparations for a systematic, harmonious change. He called two of the trustees, W.J. Clark, a Los Angeles businessman, and his closest friend, Ernest A. Kilbourne, who came to America six months before Charles' Home-call. He laid the bank books with his last signature in their hands, and the Lord lifted the burden from his shoulders.

He wrote in his diary:

> My heart is kept in perfect peace as I lay down the work which has been so dear to me. It was God who raised the work up, enlarging it year after year; it was God who supplied its great need for 21 unbroken years; and God, our infinitely rich Treasurer, is still leading the band. As he was with us in the yesterdays, so will he be with us in the tomorrows – the God of the changing years. The

work is his, not ours, and because of that fact, it cannot fail. Luther, in the day of his great crisis, cried out, "Lord, Thou art imperiled with us." God has enabled us to lay the foundations, to "lengthen thy cords, and strengthen thy stakes" (Isaiah 54:2), and although it shall not be my privilege to be upon earth, mingling with the reapers in garnering the harvest, I shall look over the battlements of heaven and shout to my fellow workers now and again, "Sail on! Sail on!" Lovingly I turn it over into his hand, the pierced hand, the safe hand. I trust him utterly.

There seemed to be a peculiar completeness to his days. He had no anxiety about the future of the work, as it was wholly committed into the hand of God. Charles gave this word of admonition to those left behind:

"I am so convinced that the work is God's that nothing from without can by any means harm it, but you must stay close together and at the foot of the cross, where there is none of self but all of Christ. You can harm it if you allow disunity among yourselves, looking after your own personal interests and failing to be true to the vision God has given us. Read Psalm 133 often. 'There the LORD commanded the blessing.' Have fervent love among yourselves. Pray for fresh baptisms of love. Disunity cannot live in an atmosphere of love."

At that time, prominent missionaries stated that The Oriental Missionary Society was better equipped with national leaders than any other mission in Asia, with more than 1,000 national preachers. So, Charles Cowman could thoroughly commit the work so dear to him into their hands. Afterward, it was said of him, "Insofar as Charles Cowman's successful achievements may be traced to the correctness of policy, what is known as statesmanship, we believe he should be credited with missionary genius of the highest order."

Chapter 15

In the Thickening Shadows

Charles' suffering had been acute for several weeks; the muscles of his heart were fast losing tone. A few penciled notes in his diary tell some of his thoughts after he met with the Lord on July 15, 1924: "It looks as if the Lord has forbidden my return to the Orient. He was peculiarly present with me this morning about daybreak. Just what he meant to tell me, I am not certain. It may have been my healing, or it may be that he was trying to tell me that the time of my departure is at hand. I would rather remain upon earth a while longer, if it is his will, but if he wants me in his presence, I can only say, 'Thy will be done.'"

The King of Kings was giving him a call. He could not clearly interpret the summons at first. The day following we could scarcely speak to each other, as an unspeakable burden rested upon our hearts. He sat quietly by his desk and penned the lines that he could not speak. He was willing to go, but leaving me was the crucial test. However, when the hour arrived, God's great arms of love tenderly folded about him and gave him marvelous grace.

It is hard to allow others into our bereavement, and I hesitated to share excerpts of his last messages; however, at the request of friends, I have done so.

> July 16, 1924. I thank God for you, my loved one, as for no other gift of his bestowing. You cannot know what you are to me; no words will express it. God's blessings to me have been very marked, and I desire to rear a memorial to him for his love and tender care over me, since I left all to follow him. Everything in our lives has gone like the unwinding of a golden thread.
>
> You will have no one but God after I am gone, my dearest, so "lean hard upon God." As you enter the pathway of heart-loneliness, he will give grace and comfort.
>
> The work will need your ministry as never before. Dedicate yourself to it anew and keep close to Jesus. Complete my work and yours. The Lord has raised you up to be a witness to the ends of the earth. After a time, you should go to Asia and see how our brethren are doing. Encourage their hearts and strengthen their hands. They will need you there. Live in Japan awhile and keep in close fellowship with dear Brother Nakada. I dearly love him.
>
> Do your utmost for the evangelization of China. See to it that the Bible training schools are established. That is God's method. Let nothing turn you aside from it. I have prayed through for these schools, so just follow the Lord as he leads step by step, and his plan will unfold and funds will be

given. *Jehovah-Jireh.* Hold fast to the old truths and walk in the old paths. Be brave, dear heart!

After my departure, you will have to find comfort first of all, before you can administer it. Read 1 Thessalonians 4:14–18 often. God will comfort in his own appointed way, which is to watch for his appearing and the resurrection of those who sleep in him. I would not advise you to spend too much time at my grave, as it will only keep the wound open. I will not be there, you know. The Lord will bring you triumphantly through. He assured me yesterday that he would, and there will be the sweetest reunion in the Summerland.

You will be all alone when the beauty of the summer is gone, but there is an eternal summer, heaven, that will be exceedingly beautiful, and we shall dwell together there.

Don't let the song go out of your life, my love, for your sake, for others' sake, and maybe I too shall hear it and be glad.

Over the real romance of our lives, over the tenderest, loveliest passages in his letters, a veil must be thrown, but it will not be lifting it too far to say that Charles Cowman fulfilled the ideal of a most true and perfect husband to the one woman blessed with a love that never failed. He wrote his letter literally with tears, which bears impressive witness to the deep affection for me, as I now wait on the earth side.

On the evening of July 17, the Master whispered to us both, "Tonight I am going to lead you through the valley of the shadow." It was as real as if he had stepped into the room in bodily form and spoken to us.

Charles called for a little group of his very dear friends to come quickly. Among them were Ernest A. Kilbourne, W.J. Clark, and A.N. Clark. When they entered the room, he said, "I wish to see you and bid you farewell." He thanked them for their ministry of love. To Brother Kilbourne he said, "What comrades we have been throughout the years! Our hearts have been knit together – no, *knit* is not the word; our hearts were *burned* together. What glorious time we have had out in Asia! I have no regret that my life is slipping away because of what I have done for my Asian brothers. I am glad, oh, so glad!"

He gave a message to each, then a word for all the national workers. None were forgotten. He sent words of appreciation and love to friends in England who had stood nobly by the work for more than 20 years. To greatly loved holiness leaders, he sent the messages "Press on" and "Walk in love as dear children," and to the "Revivalist Family," he sent special thanks for their outpoured love throughout the years of his missionary career. To the trustees, he sent special love; to his greatly loved friend Charles E. Sawtelle, he sent a word of tender thanks. And to The Oriental Missionary Society family scattered throughout the earth, he sent a loving farewell message, exhorting them to press the battle to the gates until Jesus comes.

Following the farewells came plans for the work so dear to him. It will take years to completely execute the plans so clear in his mind to the very last. Complete suggestions were left for those who were to take up the work where he left off. How beautifully God arranged it that Brother Kilbourne could be near him during his last six months upon earth!

The entire evening was glorious. Now and then he would shout out, "I feel so clean! The blood of Jesus cleanseth me from all sin!" God did not permit sadness to overwhelm us; on the contrary, all experienced a lifting spirit, and none could shed a tear. It seemed like a farewell service to some missionary who was bound for a far-off climate, and we were standing on the shore waving him off.

There came sweet peace to our hearts, and we knew that the Master had a great work to be done by his death that could not have been accomplished in any other way. We do not know what or how, perhaps never shall, but it is even so. Charles was calling back to us that the end was worth all his toil. What a wonderful thing to shout back from the grave and say, "I have not a regret. It was worth it all." We felt as if we had been on the Mount of Transfiguration and had caught a glimpse of Paradise through the Gates Ajar.

For more than two hours, Charles talked until he seemed satisfied. He then turned to me and said, "I must now bid you goodbye, the last one of all." It was a beautiful, peaceful, loving parting, and God did not fail us in giving great grace. After this farewell, he said, "Now I am ready to go. Please Jesus, take me at Thy moment." We looked on with breathless awe as he started down the valley, and there came a conscious moment when each one felt he had taken the last step with him.

Being very weary, he pillowed his head on his chair, as he had not been able to lie down in many months. And he slept quietly there, in perfect peace, throughout the night. When the day dawned, he was still upon earth, but the Charles Cowman we knew was changed. He lived and breathed but did not belong to this world.

On the night of July 17, a stroke paralyzed his entire left side, and the doctor said he could live only a few hours, but he lingered in that low valley for several weeks. His suffering was keen. Often he was delirious, preaching to dear ones in Asia. Again and again, the words of Scripture came to us in the day watches and the night watches throughout September: "And sitting down they watched him there" (Matthew 27:36). It was about all we could do. Singing was all that we could do to help him rest while the dear, great heart was ebbing out to sea. The old, familiar hymns soothed and quieted amid the eruptions of pain.

On September 23, his friend W.J. Clark brought to us an exquisite, night-blooming cereus. It had reached perfection that very night, and the sight of that fragile but beautiful flower that blooms only once and then dies when it has reached its height of beauty spoke volumes to our hearts, but there was an inbreathed peace.

Wednesday, September 24, was a typical California day. The hills and dales were clothed with life and beauty with a few fleecy clouds in the bright heavens. The birds sang as if the world had no grief in it. In hundreds of towns, villages, and hamlets in Japan and Korea, people were wending their way to churches that he had been instrumental in giving to them. Many of the dear people had never seen his face and little realized how blessing and salvation had come to them, because for a quarter of a century he had planned, prayed, and worked with their faces mirrored in his heart and with their salvation uppermost in his mind. They went to their houses of worship while their friend and missionary was gradually sinking into the sleep that has no earthly waking.

Slowly, the sun went down. Twilight fell and deepened into a perfect autumn evening. We watched and waited until the midnight hour. Ebbing out to sea – dear, great heart! He looked the picture of peace. How we yearned that he might be able to tell us when he caught sight of heaven's glory! The clock tolled half past twelve, the eternal gates were open, and all weariness, the pain, the watchings, and the fastings were passed. He had reached Home. His warfare was accomplished. God had lifted his cross and given him his crown.

I knew that my earthly anchor was gone, that the little brown home in the west was henceforth only a house and not a home; I was alone. "It was too painful for me; until I went into the sanctuary of God" (Psalm 73:16–17).

Those passing by the home did not notice the thick, black crepe, symbolic of mourning, but rather a bouquet of lovely flowers; they knew that the *smiling invalid* had slipped Home. As Charles wished, there were no tokens of death visible. He requested that his relatives not wear mourning clothes and that I should wear white, for he said, "It will be my coronation day, and why should you be dressed in black, which symbolizes death."

His memorial service was held in Trinity Missionary Church, a church he had helped to pray into existence, and one he greatly loved, as it was a vibrant missionary church. It was in this pulpit that he had delivered his last missionary message. At the conclusion, someone had started the grand old hymn:

> All hail the power of Jesus' name,
> Let angels prostrate fall
> Bring forth the royal diadem,
> And crown Him Lord of all.[22]

Such triumphant praise burst from every heart that it seemed as if the whole world must have caught the echo. All present had sensed something heavenly.

The funeral service was exceedingly simple. Friends who came from surrounding towns and suburbs filled the church. The Reverend Joseph H. Smith, president of the National Holiness Association and a warm friend of Charles', had charge of the service. Two of Charles' favorite hymns were sung, "Christ Returneth" and "Home of the Soul."

Brother Kilbourne attempted to speak about his departed

---

22 Edward Perronet, "All Hail the Power of Jesus' Name," 1779.

comrade but could not finish as the heart-wound had been too deep. He read the telegrams and cablegrams from many distant friends in Japan, Korea, and China. It seemed more like a rousing missionary service than a funeral service. To many, the Word came with fresh meaning: "There is no death" for "death is swallowed up in victory" (1 Corinthians 15:54).

One speaker said, "If someone asks, 'Why did he die?' I would reply, 'I cannot tell.' I can only say that God knows when men ought to die. It would seem wise to leave the matter with him. Some life tasks are completed in a few quick, pulsating years, and the laborer may fitly rest. Some can only be accomplished in the course of a long, weary struggle. Others must traverse 'the great way around,' while some may take a direct pathway to the goal. But God knows. It is not how long a man lives that counts; it is what he puts into life while he is living. Charles has lived about three times longer than any other missionary of his generation, for he surely put into the last twenty-five years three times as much as an ordinary worker. His name is on the honor roll of the world's history. The faithful warrior is home today, 'waiting for the morning.'"

The body was taken to beautiful Hollywood Cemetery and laid in the shadow of a great cypress tree. At the graveside, Rev. Smith said, "A precious worker has been removed from our midst, and the responsibility has fallen upon us to stand in the breach and fill up the gap. More than ever do we need to pray for the work that this dear brother has laid down. Let us give ourselves afresh to the work; let us pledge ourselves to pray for it. God bless the Society bereft of its founder and raise up scores of young men and women to step into the breach."

Immediately, friends wrote, "By all means let us have a memorial to him. But where? Not in a painted window nor a great pile of stone, but out in China, a Bible training institute where the prayers of his suffering years will have an answer."

Two days after the funeral, a letter came addressed to him. It was from a fellow worker who did not yet know of his translation. It read, "Dear Brother Cowman: My heart is burdened over China, and I wish to do something to assist you. I will send $25,000 soon for the construction of the Bible training institute."

How I wished that it had been received earlier. But I am sure the Lord would never have kept it from Charles, and into my sore heart came a consciousness that he knew and that there was rejoicing in heaven.

In September 1925, one year later, The Oriental Missionary Society rose up to follow its beckoning Lord, and the work was launched in China. If you had visited Shanghai, you would have found a beautiful compound of three acres covered with buildings. On the cornerstone of the chapel these words were inscribed:

THE COWMAN MEMORIAL

BIBLE TRAINING INSTITUTE

Chapter 16

The Afterglow of a Sunlit Life

In the nine years after Charles was summoned into the presence of the King, thousands of people read the pages of the original *Missionary Warrior*. The cause of world evangelization received a mighty forward momentum. The work of OMS was viewed as a model for missions that generated the call to a forward march for hundreds of other societies in every part of the world. Charles' slogan, "A trained national ministry, self-supporting national churches, the Gospel to every creature," was caught by thousands.

In 1932, the Depression deeply affected the whole world. Funds were scarce and the gifts that flowed into the missionary treasury were small, so the Koreans were informed at their yearly convention that the 24 graduates of the Bible Training Institute who had expected to open new stations would be unable to do so. The Enemy of souls sat by that empty treasury and boldly declared, "Now the work will fail, for I have power to close doors and to lock up funds."

But Another also sat "over against the treasure" – the One with whom nothing is impossible.

Prayer was made without ceasing; for hours, a steady stream

of intercession went up to the throne. They refused to be denied. They held on in faith until they believed the answer was on the way; then they sang praises until the hall echoed with their shouts. They had prayed through.

The answer could not be delayed. Out of their deep poverty they came and laid gifts on the offering plate, which was altogether too small to hold their contributions for the work of the Lord. At a time of year when the weather was cold, men took off their warm, wool overcoats and carried them to the platform as an offering. Leather shoes, briefcases, watches, spectacles, blankets – every available thing that these dear people possessed – were freely given. Hundreds of women of the congregation took from their hair the one silver pin that held their long, dark tresses together and put these pins in the offering. One precious little Bible woman whose station was 340 miles away in the mountains walked down the aisle and laid her return railway ticket on the offering plate. She would gladly walk home, for the joy of the Lord was her strength. Owners of an acre or two of land or a yoke of oxen gave them joyfully.

This "giving meeting" began at 2:00 in the afternoon and continued until after 10:00 that night, when a missionary, with his heart near breaking, went to the platform and commanded them to give no more. He said, "I can bear it no longer." Thus the sacrificial but enthusiastic giving was brought to a close, and with great joy, the Korean saints departed to their homes.

The convention closed in a flood of blessing. All the workers returned to their stations, and the 24 graduates were sent to new districts far inland. The offerings were quickly converted into money, which amounted to nearly $3,500.

After such times we felt as though we had been filling ourselves with spiritual oxygen, and we were exhilarated and refreshed. There was something Pauline in their faith, something Elijah-like in their confidence in prayer, and something Napoleonic in their audacity.

That year of depression was one of the greatest years in the history of the Society to that point. Not a station was closed, not a worker sent away. On the contrary, 132 new stations were opened.

On a radiant day in 1933, these lines were penned in the missionary house of The Oriental Missionary Society, Shanghai, China:

> "The Cowman Memorial Bible Training Institute, the first unit of a chain of five planned for China, opened in 1925, the year after Charles' Homegoing. Great numbers of precious Chinese men and women had received training and were out gathering the great white harvest."

Down in South China, in Canton, one of the world's largest cities, the second unit had been given in answer to prayer. There, at the very heart of a population of more than 100 million souls, the Bible Training Institute was established to train the Cantonese to reach their own people.

China's old capital city, Peking, North China, is one of the most fascinating cities in the world and boasts a history of more than 4,500 years. A large gateway stood in that city, over which hung this sign: THE ORIENTAL MISSIONARY SOCIETY BIBLE TRAINING INSTITUTE. This is the Society's third unit in China, which opened in September 1932. God gave us 14 old palace buildings of purely Chinese architecture, arranged to the minutest detail, for our institute. The old ancestral hall served as a splendid chapel, and the various buildings easily accommodated 150 students. After just one year in existence, a number of fine Mandarin-speaking Chinese had already heard the Master's call to follow him.

Though dead, Charles Cowman still spoke. Five monuments, more lasting than brass and more precious than gold, stood to his memory in the centers of three great nations, lifting high the flaming light of a testimony that flashed its beams over the Far East.

Finis cannot be affixed to this added chapter of *Missionary Warrior* without a note of personal praise to the One who has been so faithful to me. In the spring of 1933, something beautiful happened – no, not *happened*, for it was *planned* by none other than the loving Lord himself for her who pens these lines.

On the day of Charles' coronation, September 25, 1924, this promise was definitely given to me: "Said I not unto thee, that, if thou wouldest believe, thou shouldest see the glory of God?" (John 11:40). For nearly nine years, I pondered over that word and often asked my Lord to reveal to me its meaning. At last, the answer was given.

It came at twilight when the huge tent on our Japan compound was filled with believers for the evening service. It had been a busy day. There was only one secluded spot where one could withdraw from the crowds and be quite alone, and that wee corner was the garden at the rear of my old, sweet home. Often in years past, I had gone to that little spot with Charles to watch the setting sun, as it had been our custom to spend those few moments together at the close of each day.

On this particular evening, the atmosphere was so clear that the mountains stood out in bold relief. Not a cloud floated across the heavens. Some moments before, the great red ball had dropped behind the distant range. Then came the memories! The evening was an exact replica of the one long ago when, together in the heart of the Hakone Mountains, we watched the sunset. For one brief moment, the heart cried out for "the touch of a vanished hand, And the sound of a voice that is still!"[23] Ah, *human* comfort! None but the loving Lord himself is great enough for loneliness.

A voice softly whispered, "Look up! Look up!" Instantly, I obeyed, and there in the distance I saw Japan's loveliest mountain bathed in a color as soft and dainty as springtime blossoms. Gradually, the soft color changed to a deep crimson, rivers of glory wound through meadows of gold, and there in the lavish glory of the sunset – the faint foreshadowing of the glory of the Father's House – I watched the exquisitely beautiful afterglow.

It was an hour for retrospection. Time turned backward, and together with my loved one, I was once more walking over mountains and vales, seeking the "other sheep." Then this question stole into my mind unbidden. Had Charles received his Home-call too early? Had death robbed him of his inheritance as a missionary? Was Charles Cowman defeated because he finished his course years ahead of his time? A thousand times, no! The torch that he bore aloft was not quenched; it continued to shine with all the brilliance of the sun, and thousands took that torch from his hand and carried it aloft into every corner of Japan, Korea, and China.

My reverie was broken by the sound of a bell. It was time for the evening service to begin. Entering the tent, I saw a never-to-be-forgotten scene. The crowds! The crowds! On the long platform were 100 national preachers; many of them had been with the Society since its inception. Faithful men! Hundreds in the audience were delegates and workers from the 935 outstations. They represented the Russian work in China, the Korean work in Japan, and the stations along the Manchurian border. The Ainu brother was there from the cold northland, and the converted headhunter from the Formosan jungle. A dusky-faced Celebes Islander was there also.

---

23   Alfred, Lord Tennyson, ""Break, Break, Break," 1835.

As I entered the tent, the vast throng was standing with hands uplifted while they sang:

> Amazing grace, how sweet the sound
> That saved a wretch like me!
> I once was lost, but now am found,
> Was blind, but now I see.
>
> Through many dangers, toils and snares,
> I have already come;
> 'Tis grace hath brought me safe thus far,
> And grace will lead me home.
>
> When we've been there ten thousand years,
> Bright shining as the sun,
> We've no less days to sing God's praise
> Than when we'd first begun.[24]

This glorious company of saints, keeping time to the music with uplifted hands, reminded me of a great field of golden grain, waving to and fro in the summer breeze. I do not expect ever to witness a lovelier sight. But, where did this golden harvest come from?

From a single buried grain.

"Except a corn of wheat fall into the ground and die, it abideth alone: but if it die, it bringeth forth much fruit" (John 12:24).

I heard again that precious promise: "Said I not unto thee, that, if thou wouldest believe, thou shouldest see the glory of God?" And then, yes, I understood its meaning. At that moment, I beheld *another* afterglow – the afterglow of the beautiful, laid-down life of Charles Cowman, missionary warrior.

---

24   John Newton, "Amazing Grace," 1779.

And I heard a voice from heaven saying unto me, Write, Blessed are the dead which die in the Lord from henceforth: Yea, saith the Spirit, that they may rest from their labours; and their works do follow them. – Revelation 14:13

Epilogue

Consistency, steadfastness, and a restive reaching out for souls were indeed the hallmarks of Charles Cowman. They continue to characterize the mission he founded, The Oriental Missionary Society, which became OMS International in 1973, and then One Mission Society in 2010.

Dropping the word *Oriental* from its name was in itself a testimony to the continuity of the driving spirit of its founder. He loved Asia passionately and burned himself out with fierce abandon in his insatiable hunger for the salvation of the people of Asia. However, Charles Cowman's vision extended farther than just the Far East – his was a global dream. And so, inspired by his vision and compelled by his forceful example, OMS has steadily widened its arenas of ministry into many parts of the world. Today, nearly 500 missionaries and thousands of coworkers around the world are engaged in bringing souls to Christ in more than 70 countries.

As OMS was beginning ministry in the early 1900s, Cowman developed a threefold mission strategy of evangelism, church planting, and leadership training. Through the years, OMS has modified and adjusted this strategy to fit the changing environment of modern missions. But today, the emphasis of OMS in the 21st century is essentially the same as Cowman's vision at the beginning of the 20th century.

By God's grace and with his enablement, we will seek to:

- Make multiplying disciples – Believing that the power of the Gospel in the hands of disciple-makers will transform the nations, we invest intentionally and strategically in discipleship.

- Multiply churches – We establish Christ-centered, worshiping communities of local churches capable of reproducing themselves.

- Multiply leaders – We develop leaders who can help grow other generations of leaders.

- Multiply missionary movements – We nurture missionary-sending movements from anywhere to anywhere, focusing as much as possible on those who haven't yet heard of Christ.

One Mission Society, in obedience to the Lord and in keeping faith with our founders, is committed to utilize its every opportunity to move ahead as aggressively and as far as God makes possible to help bring to reality that spectacular day seen in a vision by the apostle John:

> "After this I beheld, and, lo, a great multitude, which no man could number, of all nations, and kindreds, and people, and tongues, stood before the throne, and before the Lamb." – Revelation 7:9

Photos

Charles E. Cowman

Charles Cowman, age 15

Lettie Burd before she married Charles Cowman

Charles and Lettie Cowman shortly after their wedding, 1889

Charles and Lettie Cowman
soon after their arrival in Japan

Charles Cowman

Charles Cowman at his desk in Tokyo

The Cowmans with guests in their home in Tokyo

One of the Cowmans' prayer cards

E.A. Kilbourne and his family

Juji Nakada and his family. His mother was one of the earliest Christians in Japan.

Other Similar Titles

Another Valley, Another Victory, by Valetta Steel Crumley

Tragedy is timeless and universal. So is victory, which is defined by the author's life as letting God have the controls – allowing him to expose previously hidden beauty, now displayed for the sake of others. This inspiring life story has moved countless others to overcome and look at adversity from God's perspective. When viewed from the top, a valley is precious and beautiful.

Valetta lost her young son Danny to leukemia; her husband Henry succumbed to Hodgkin's disease a few years later; then she lost her remaining two children in a tragic car accident. Her new reality was nearly unbearable, but when offered a secure position in her father's business, Valetta refused. The Lord had called her and Henry into ministry, and there was a mountain of unfinished business.

Today, Valetta has traveled the world, sharing Christ and teaching Christians how to share Christ in their communities. Thousands have been saved, and countless more inspired in their walk with the Lord. Valetta's story will touch you, move you, and challenge you to let God do as he desires in and through your life, enabling you to minister to others in ways you never would have imagined possible.

Available where books are sold.

Expendable for God, by Pedro Gutiérrez

Don Pedro's story highlights the necessity of preaching God's Word to those in need of moral and social regeneration. His ministry as a pastor and an evangelist is an outstanding model of selfless, loving dedication and proven leadership. His courageous, yet tender responses to victims of sin and deception will impress all who read the record of his life.

His seventy years of faithfulness to Christ give us a beautiful and almost unparalleled pattern for today's ministers of the truth. From the beginning, Don Pedro had a particular appeal for young people. Read here of how he dealt with personal concerns, how he handled issues of family and church, and how he carried out the great mission of his life – introducing men and women to the Savior and nurturing them in the Scriptures.

His warm and transparent friendship, modest lifestyle, and caring spirit still draw us closer to the sovereign Lord who, in His grace, blessed Colombia and regions beyond through this God-fearing *giant from Quindio.*

Available where books are sold.

No Reserves, No Retreats, No Regrets, **by En Erny**

My life story begins with a preacher who, by the leading of the Spirit, refused to end a service until my father, a successful businessman, had given his heart to the Lord. I eventually followed in my father's footsteps into full-time ministry, but only after overcoming self-doubt and self-consciousness in my ability to share the gospel.

God took that doubt away when a young man gave his heart to the Lord after I told him about Jesus. From that moment on, in Taiwan, the Philippines, and other places where I served, I saw the tremendous hand of the Lord at work as I allowed Him to lead and work through me. My desire is that you will be inspired and motivated to serve the Lord as freely and willingly as I was privileged to do for many years. May you, by God's grace, determine to live with no reserves, no retreats, and no regrets.

Available where books are sold.

www.ingramcontent.com/pod-product-compliance
Lightning Source LLC
Chambersburg PA
CBHW060524080526
44586CB00012B/600